CITIZEN COMEDY IN THE AGE OF SHAKESPEARE

ALEXANDER LEGGATT

Citizen Comedy in the Age of Shakespeare

UNIVERSITY OF TORONTO PRESS

© University of Toronto Press 1973
Toronto and Buffalo
Printed in Canada

ISBN 0-8020-5288-6
LC 73-76128

For Clifford Leech

Contents

Acknowledgments

The present study began as a PH D thesis for the Shakespeare Institute, and my first debt of gratitude is to those who helped me at that stage. Eric Pendry and Peter Davison were patient and painstaking advisers, and I also profited from consultation with the Institute's Director, T.J.B. Spencer, with Stanley Wells, and with three of my fellow students (as they then were) who were working on related projects: Doug Sedge, Alan Somerset, and Gordon Williams.

In making the revision, I have had the advice of Clifford Leech, J.M.R. Margeson, and Brian Parker, not to mention the anonymous readers for the University of Toronto Press, all of whom have commented, helpfully and in detail, on the manuscript at its various stages. I have been saved from much folly and error, and led to explore important material I would otherwise have neglected; I am deeply grateful to all concerned. The follies, errors, and omissions that remain are, of course, my own responsibility.

I would also like to thank the librarians of the Shakespeare Institute and of the Nuffield Library at Stratford-on-Avon, who have been unfailingly helpful; and Molly Goodeve, Kitty Page, and Philippa Simpson, who have at various stages produced clear typescript out of chaos.

Finally, since money is an important theme in this book, I am glad to acknowledge three debts of a more material kind. The Canada Council provided a research grant that allowed me to spend a summer in re-reading and re-writing. The book has been published with the help of a grant from the Humanities Research Council of Canada, using funds provided by the Canada Council, and with the help of the Publications Fund of the University of Toronto Press.

ALEXANDER LEGGATT
June 1973

CITIZEN COMEDY IN THE AGE OF SHAKESPEARE

NOTE

All references to plays are to the editions listed in section (a) of the Bibliography; where there are no line numbers, page numbers have been given. In quoting from these editions, spelling and punctuation have been modernized.

Unless otherwise stated, information given about the dates and auspices of the plays is based on Alfred Harbage's *Annals of English Drama 975–1700*, revised by Samuel Schoenbaum (London, 1964).

1
Introduction

'Citizen comedy' is one of those conveniently vague terms that seem serviceable enough until an attempt is made to define them. A general idea of the sort of play one has in mind (*Eastward Ho* rather than *Twelfth Night*) may do for casual references, but the reader of an extended study of citizen comedy in the age of Shakespeare will want a more exact sense of what the term means to the writer. For this writer it means comedy set in a predominantly middle-class social milieu. That definition, however, raises the considerable problem of defining the middle class. Shopkeepers, merchants, and craftsmen who are rich enough to employ the labour of other men fit easily enough into this category, and usually are clearly identified as such in the drama. There are, however, other figures, such as Ford and Page in *The Merry Wives of Windsor*, who, without having specific occupations which would help us to place them on the social scale, seem to occupy a middle station – high enough to have comfortable homes, but too low to be called aristocrats. Still others (like Middleton's gallants), though they belong to the landed gentry, live and operate in a citizen environment, and (such was the flexibility of social classes at the time) have close relatives in that environment.

It is most convenient, then, to define the social milieu of citizen comedy by exclusion. I have selected plays which do not deal predominantly with the court or the aristocracy, but with the fluid, often ill-defined area that lies between this and the lowest class of workmen, servants, rogues, and vagabonds. I have also applied a check which, though it has nothing to do with defining the genre, is intended to keep the discussion within reasonable limits. I am dealing only with plays set in England. This is because, as I will explain in a moment, I am most interested in comedies depicting contemporary social situations – situations the audience themselves might be expected to face – and I feel, as Ben Jonson came to feel, that this can be done most effectively by using a native setting, to which the audience can clearly relate. Two exceptions have been made: *The Honest Whore*, because its Bedlam and Bridewell scenes give it a definite local reference despite its ostensibly Italian setting; and the Cambridge comedy *Club Law*, in which Athens is a very thin disguise for the English university town. The discussion has also been restricted to plays which can reasonably be dated between 1585 and 1625. Jonson's *The Staple of News*, being a major writer's clearest attempt to deal with two of the commonest themes of the genre, prodigality and usury, has been allowed to slip in, though it really belong to the early months of 1626.

Three things should be noticed at once about the collection of plays I have just isolated. First, while these plays are written *about* the middle class, they are not necessarily written *for* them. There are exceptions (the citizen-heroes of Dekker and Heywood come to mind), but more often than not the angle from which middle-class characters and situations are portrayed is not determined primarily by the special interests of that class, or of any other. The second point is connected with the first: sometimes class borders are carefully drawn within the plays, so that it becomes important to recognize that we are dealing with citizens, or gentry, or a collision between the two – sometimes, but not always. Often the fluid social group I have attempted to describe will be used to dramatize broad social issues that do not depend on class only. Finally, the category 'citizen comedy' cuts across a variety of comic modes: we find ourselves dealing with the satiric, the didactic, and the simply amusing, with everything from lightweight farce to pieces that verge on domestic drama.

So far this sounds like a recipe for critical confusion, and the question arises, why bother? One answer is that there *is* a common factor in these plays, an interest in practical social issues: how to get money, and how to spend it; how to get a wife, and how to keep her. This is connected with the social milieu of the plays: the action is often stylized, but the settings are prosaic and familiar – streets, shops, private houses. The characters enter forests only occasionally and courts hardly at all (Simon Eyre does not go to the King; the King comes to him). Courtship and romance, the driving motives of Shakespearean comedy, are underplayed here. Young lovers, when present at all, have to make their way in a world of hard bargaining, and it is the bargaining more than the love that commands our attention. This range of interest is still fairly broad, but it is at least clearly defined, and makes of citizen comedy a body of material sufficiently coherent to be worth discussing. In particular, the issues of money and sex, and their frequent interaction, will concern us throughout the following chapters.

The standard approach would have been to examine major authors in succession, but this creates problems in dealing with Elizabethan comedy, since so many significant plays are anonymous or collaborative works (experience shows that in a book with chapters on Chapman, Jonson, and Marston, *Eastward Ho* gets lost and wanders among the footnotes). It is easy also to lose sight of the rich, varied background provided by lesser known writers, and the loss is twofold: the achievements of the major figures can be more clearly appreciated when compared with conventional work; and the minor figures often have achievements of their own to offer, which have been unjustly neglected. Here, instead, the plays have been approached through the treatment of those social issues that seem to be the common factor in them – bearing in mind that a comedy can hardly ever be a simple social tract, and that its tension and energy will depend not on ideas alone but on the interaction of social concern with the requirements and opportunities of comic form.

The approach taken in this study puts chronology to one side, and it might be useful to provide here a brief survey of the main lines of development in citizen comedy for the reader (if he feels the need of it) to use as a road map in the next few chapters. The antecedents of citizen comedy are mixed, to say the least. The basic pattern of New Comedy – an intrigue in which a young man plots against an old one to gain money, or the girl of his choice, or both[1] – was familiar not only from Plautus and Terence but from the comedy of the Italian Renaissance, which added to it a rival-wooer motif (usually a young man against an old one) and a preoccupation with domestic themes, with jealous husbands and Patient Griselda figures.[2] This type of comedy found its way to England fairly early in the sixteenth century, and there are many instances of English writers, particularly at universities, producing Italianate comedies.[3] The conflict of youth and age, the intrigue based on money and sex, were thus part of a long and vital continental tradition. English drama, in the low-life scenes of the miracle plays, had displayed its own interest in ordinary people and domestic settings. This interest continued in such early comedies as *Gammer Gurton's Needle* (*c.* 1553) and *Tom Tyler and his Wife* (*c.*1560). Such motifs

---

1 See Northrop Frye, *The Anatomy of Criticism* (Princeton, 1957), pp. 44, 163–5.
2 See R. Warwick Bond, *Early Plays from the Italian* (Oxford, 1911), p. xli, and Marvin T. Herrick, *Italian Comedy in the Renaissance* (Urbana, 1960), *passim*.
3 See Bond, *Early Plays, passim*, and F.S. Boas, *University Drama in the Tudor Age* (Oxford, 1914), pp. 133–56, 286–321.

as the shrew and the rival wooers, basic material in European comedy, were well established in the native tradition.[4] The later English morality plays also became concerned with social rather than religious issues, attacking such abuses as usury and corrupt justice.[5] The characters even shed some of their abstraction, becoming recognizeable social types, with specific occupations and clear places on the social scale.[6] An interest in the citizen class in particular can be seen in the chronicle plays of the 1590s, which often glorify this class and celebrate its value to the commonwealth.[7] There are several examples of citizens who are on the best of terms with the monarch, usually through performing deeds of patriotic valour.[8]

This by no means exhausts the list of possible antecedents – in chapter 3, for example, we shall notice the importance of continental plays on the theme of the prodigal – but it may at least serve to indicate the complexity of the background against which citizen comedy was written. Social concern, class awareness, sexual and financial intrigue, domestic settings – all were ready to be shaped and used by the individual playwright in his own way. That way, of course, was often very individual indeed, posing a severe problem for the critic who tries to set up categories. All the same, a few main lines of development may be sketched, without doing too much damage to the complexity of the situation (and, I might add, without making too much depend on our very shaky knowledge of the exact dates of plays).

In the 1590s, only a few plays can be classed as citizen comedies; plays with more exotic settings and more romantic themes appear to have occupied the attention of the public; native subjects were largely represented by chronicle

---

4 The shrew is found, for example, in *Tom Tyler and his Wife* (c. 1560) and John Heywood's *Johan Johan, Tyb his Wife and Sir Johan* (c. 1520); the rival wooers, in Nicholas Udall's *Ralph Roister Doister* (c. 1552), and in several mummers' plays: see Charles Read Baskervill, 'Mummers' Wooing Plays in England,' *MP*, xxi (February 1924), 225–72.

5 See, for example, George Wapull, *The Tide Tarrieth No Man* (1576), and Thomas Lupton, *All for Money* (c. 1577). This development is discussed by Louis B. Wright, 'Social Aspects of Some Belated Moralities,' *Anglia*, liv (1930), 107–48.

6 Some examples may be found in *The Tide Tarrieth No Man*, W. Wager's *Enough is as Good as a Feast* (c. 1560), and *A Knack to Know a Knave* (1592). This growing concreteness means that some plays, such as those of Robert Wilson, dwell in a border area between morality plays and ordinary drama.

7 See Louis B. Wright, *Middle-Class Culture in Elizabethan England* (Chapel Hill, 1935), pp. 623–4.

8 See, for example, *The Life and Death of Jack Straw* (auspices unknown, c. 1591), and *Edward IV*, possibly by Thomas Heywood (Derby's c. 1599). There are also some unflattering portraits of the citizen class – in, for example, *The Weakest Goeth to the Wall* (Oxford's, c. 1600), and *A Larum for London* (Chamberlain's, c. 1599) – but by and large they are depicted with sympathy and approval.

plays. There were, however, a few comedies dealing with ordinary English life. In the earlier years of the decade, these keep to the rustic setting first exploited by *Gammer Gurton's Needle*. The themes, as in Henry Porter's *The Two Angry Women of Abington* (Admiral's, c. 1588) and Shakespeare's *The Merry Wives of Windsor* (Chamberlain's, 1597),[9] are domestic, dealing with the problems of marriage, and the tone is generally good tempered. *The Merry Wives* in particular shows strong Italian influence, notably in the rival-wooers subplot.[10] It has been suggested that Shakespeare is remodelling an earlier play, more thoroughly Italianate,[11] but the evidence that has been brought forward merely suggests Shakespeare's great debt to Italian comedy, and does not establish that this must be accounted for by revision of an early work.

It has also been suggested that the earlier play (if there was one) was a comedy of London life.[12] It would be interesting if this could be established, for the early play would then have a strong title to being the first London comedy (a fact not remarked on by those who have made the suggestion); unfortunately the evidence is not strong.[13] The honour generally goes to William Haughton's *Englishmen for my Money* (Admiral's), which belongs to 1598[14] (the year, interestingly enough, of the first appearance of Stow's *Survey of London*). We do not know if it is really the first London comedy, because we do not know what we have lost; but London comedy it certainly is; and Haughton seems, at times, to use his local colour with the self-consciousness of an innovator. Street and other place names abound; we know where many of the characters live, and could find them on a map; we even hear, at one point, the sound of Bow Bell. The comedy is also significant for our purposes in that, like *The Merry*

9 In dating this play in the 1590s, I have accepted the suggestion of William Green, *Shakespeare's Merry Wives of Windsor* (Princeton, 1962), pp. 21–5, that the play was performed for the Garter Feast of 1597. Green's evidence is, as he himself admits, circumstantial, but it is extremely attractive.

10 The rival-wooers plot is also used by Jonson at this period in his rustic comedy *A Tale of a Tub* (Admiral's? c. 1596).

11 See Oscar James Campbell, 'The Italianate Background of *The Merry Wives of Windsor*,' *Essays and Studies in English and Comparative Literature by Members of the English Department of the University of Michigan* (Ann Arbor, 1932), pp. 81–117.

12 See A.W. Pollard and John Dover Wilson, 'The "Stolne and Surreptitious" Shakespearian Texts,' *TLS* (7 August 1919), p. 420; Sir Arthur Quiller-Couch, Introduction to the New Cambridge edition of the play (Cambridge, 1954), pp. xxii–xxiii; and Thomas Marc Parrott, *Shakespearean Comedy* (New York, 1949), p. 255.

13 The crucial piece of evidence is Dr Caius' reference to his 'counting-house,' which has led to the suggestion that the original Caius was a merchant. But a 'counting-house' could be found anywhere, and it could be an office of any sort, not necessarily a place for counting money. See Green, *Shakespeare's Merry Wives*, p. 197.

14 See E.K. Chambers, *The Elizabethan Stage* (Oxford, 1923), III, 335.

Wives, it has a plot (dealing with rival suitors) as thoroughly Italianate as its setting is thoroughly English.[15]

At the turn of the century, the interest of playwrights begins to shift towards citizen comedy; though there is no definite vogue of the sort that will develop later, more plays fit the category, and the re-opening of the private theatres adds to the number. In some cases, such as *Wily Beguiled* (Paul's? *c*. 1602) and William Haughton's *Grim the Collier of Croydon* (Admiral's? 1600), the rustic setting which dominated earlier comedy is retained; but in others London is the background of the action, and the rustic setting loses favour as the century advances. The most notable London comedy before 1604 is Thomas Dekker's *The Shoemakers' Holiday* (Admiral's, 1599). Here there is a clear line of descent from the chronicle plays mentioned earlier: the background of the French wars, and many of the characters, including Simon Eyre himself,[16] are based on history. The glorification of citizen life and, in particular, the scenes in which the king expresses friendly approval of Eyre are elements originating in the chronicle plays. The use of these chronicle features in comedy was to be copied in later years by Thomas Heywood in the Second Part of *If You Know Not Me, You Know Nobody* (Queen Anne's, 1605) and William Rowley in *A New Wonder, a Woman Never Vexed* (auspices unknown, *c*. 1625). Heywood's play, in fact, is ostensibly a chronicle, but it has grown into a citizen comedy, retaining appendages of its former state.

The interest in citizen life takes a slightly different turn in the private theatres. When they re-opened after the plague in 1604, there was a tremendous burst of activity in citizen comedy among the boys' companies. The obvious success of Dekker and Webster's *Westward Ho* (Paul's, 1604), which had begotten two sequels within a year, testifies to the popularity of such plays. Yet what the private companies offered was rather different from citizen comedy as it had been practised in the public theatre before this time. The realistic London setting, and the interest in domestic themes (particularly in *Westward Ho* and its successor, *Northward Ho* [Paul's, 1605]) were not new, but there was a new way of commenting on contemporary society. Instead of the good-tempered, easy-going manner of the earlier plays, we are offered wry, sardonic wit. The prevailing spirit is satirical.[17] Sexual behaviour and financial abuses are the prime targets, though other, more topical subjects, such as upstart

---

15 See K.M. Lea, *Italian Popular Comedy* (Oxford, 1934), II, 415–19.

16 See W.K. Chandler, 'The Sources of the Characters in *The Shoemaker's Holiday*,' *MP*, XXVII (November 1929), 175–82.

17 The development of this satiric spirit, from non-dramatic satire through Jonson's early 'comical satyres,' has been carefully traced by Brian Gibbons, *Jacobean City Comedy* (London, 1968), *passim*.

courtiers[18] and thirty-pound knights,[19] are also touched upon. There is a keen awareness of the knavery of the world, an awareness in which there is often as much relish as criticism. And this knavery is described in topical terms. It is not so much a universal quality as a symptom of the way we live now, a reflection of the passing moment. This passage from *Westward Ho* is typical:

Why there's no minute, no thought of time passes, but some villainy or other is a-brewing: why even now,now, at holding up of this finger, and before the turning down of this, some are murd'ring, some lying with their maids, some picking of pockets, some cutting purses, some cheating, some weighing out bribes. In this city some wives are cuckolding some husbands. In yonder village some farmers are now – now – grinding the jaw-bones of the poor: therefore sweet scholar, sugared Mistress Honeysuckle, take summer before you, and lay hold of it! Why, even now must you and I hatch an egg of iniquity. (II.i.185–94)

Part of this new spirit of social satire, with its topical bent, is a keener awareness of class distinctions, and a tendency to depict class warfare. It has frequently been asserted that the coterie playwrights took sides with the gentry against the citizens, and regularly mocked the latter,[20] but this is not entirely true. Some plays, like David Lord Barry's *Ram Alley* (King's Revels, c. 1608), are anti-citizen, but in *Westward Ho* and *Northward Ho* it is the gallants who are mocked, and thoroughly duped by the citizens. Middleton, the most active of the coterie writers of city comedy, is uncommitted, satirizing the follies of both sides, though he fires more often and more heavily at the citizens. On the whole, the middle classes tend to get the worst of it, but are not without their defenders in the private theatres.[21]

Many of the incidental satiric jokes in the private plays are about sex, and this topic became increasingly prominent in the plot material as well. Adultery, a favourite theme of the Italian plays, and one that had already been used in native comedy, comes to the stage with a new satiric vigour in its presentation. Plays become bawdier; prostitutes join adulterers on the comic stage. They too

18 See, for example, Thomas Middleton's *Michaelmas Term* (Paul's, c. 1606), and Edward Sharpham's *Cupid's Whirligig* (Queen's Revels, c. 1609).
19 See, for example, *Eastward Ho* (Queen's Revels, 1605), by Chapman, Jonson, and Marston.
20 See, for example, Alfred Harbage, *Shakespeare and the Rival Traditions* (New York, 1952), pp. 77, 274–7; Wright, *Middle-Class Culture*, p. 605; and M.C. Bradbrook, *The Growth and Structure of Elizabethan Comedy* (Harmondsworth, 1963), p. 54. Here as elsewhere, the difference between the two repertoires is not so rigid or so radical as Harbage's study suggests.
21 See, for example, Nathan Field's *A Woman is a Weather-cock* (Queen's Revels, c. 1609), in which the honour and personal valour of a citizen are upheld.

have a long ancestry in the New Comedy tradition; but, as is the case with adultery, there is a satiric pressure in the presentation that was not there so strongly before. There are not only more prostitutes and adulterers, but more wry, sardonic comments on prostitution and adultery.

Financial trickery, an essential feature of New Comedy, acquires a prominence on the English stage that it never had previously. This comes about largely through the work of Thomas Middleton,[22] whose intrigues tend to be based on the desire for money and land. The age-old plot devices are seen in terms of contemporary social conditions, and are made part of a sardonic commentary on greed and social climbing in the London of Middleton's day. The Plautine conflict of age and youth becomes clearer than ever before in English comedy, and is related to the class issue: Middleton depicts confrontations between young gallants and middle-aged or elderly citizens. He gives the gentry a new dramatic prominence,[23] one that they would not lose until well after the Restoration.

The private theatres between 1604 and 1610 thus offer a clear development of citizen comedy in one direction, a series of racy comedies in which satire, sex, and financial intrigue are the main ingredients. The public theatres, at the same time, are developing the genre in a different way. There are fewer plays involved, but the line of development is nonetheless clear and distinctive. While the children's comedies comment satirically on contemporary society, the adult companies offer comedies teaching moral lessons. They too comment on society but their comments are less topical, and are expressed, not with the sardonic wit of the coterie plays, but through the blunt, direct statements we associate with the moralities.

In many cases, the action is arranged to teach an erring protagonist (nearly always a prodigal) the error of his ways, and to bring him to a morally proper frame of mind. Here the debt to both the continental prodigal tradition and the early moralities is obvious. The moral basis of the play is hardly ever in doubt, and is often spelled out explicitly. At the end of the anonymous *How a Man May Choose a Good Wife From a Bad* (Worcester's, c. 1602), the hero (who

---

22 Jonson is often cited as the prime influence here, since his financial intrigue comedies are much better known. But his first play based on this idea, *Volpone*, was performed in late 1605 or early 1606, and his next, *The Alchemist*, not until 1610. Middleton's *A Trick to Catch the Old One*, *A Mad World, my Masters*, and *Michaelmas Term*, all comedies of this nature, cannot be dated precisely, but belong to the period 1604–7. There is at least a chance, therefore, that Middleton was first in the field. In any case, he was more productive in this vein; he was not influenced by Jonson any more than Jonson was by him; and he was more directly imitated by his contemporaries, such as Barry in *Ram Alley*. On the dating, see R.C. Bald, 'The Chronology of Middleton's Plays,' *MLR*, XXXII (January 1937), 33–43.

23 See Kathleen M. Lynch, *The Social Mode of Restoration Comedy* (New York, 1926), p. 28.

has tried both) places the two women on either side of him, and lectures the audience:

A good wife will be careful of her fame,
Her husband's credit, and her own good name;
And such art thou. A bad wife will respect
Her pride, her lust, and her good name neglect;
And such art thou.
...
On this hand virtue, and on this hand sin;
This who would strive to lose, or this to win? (v.iii.p.96)

How a Man May Choose is the herald of a range of plays, such as *The Fair Maid of Bristow* (King's, c. 1604) and *The London Prodigal* (King's, c. 1604),[24] in which the moral earnestness, and the grave dangers which some of the characters run, produce a seriousness of tone that takes us, at times, close to domestic tragedy; indeed, these plays have sometimes been called tragicomedies.[25]

The class issue is not raised as often or as explicitly in the public theatres as it is in the private ones. This may be because, as Alfred Harbage suggests, the dramatists at these theatres were writing for 'a general public'[26] and were therefore under no temptation to appeal to special interests. But I think it is more likely a reflection of their comparative lack of interest in topical social themes generally, and their preference for broader moral issues. On the rare occasions when the popular dramatists raise the class issue, they side with the citizens: Candido's defence of his flat cap in *The Honest Whore, Part Two*, is a case in point. Thomas Heywood, in *If You Know Not Me, You Know Nobody, Part Two*, offers a rare suggestion of class conflict: Thomas Gresham predicts that those who come to his Royal Exchange will be so impressed by the beauty of the city wives that 'Ladies shall blush to turn their vizards off, / And courtiers swear they lied when they did scoff' (p. 291). But by and large the popular theatres remain not so much impartial as indifferent to the class issue.

Heywood's comedies, written for Queen Anne's men at the Red Bull, stand apart from the rest of the popular tradition is some ways. The moral earnestness

---

24 For a detailed discussion of the influence of *How a Man May Choose*, see Arthur Hobson Quinn, Introduction to his edition of *The Fair Maid of Bristow* (Philadelphia, 1902), pp. 11–14 and p. 29; and C.R. Baskervill, 'Sources and Analogues of *How a Man May Choose a Good Wife From a Bad*,' *PMLA*, xxiv, New Series xvii (December 1909), 711–30.
25 See Marvin T. Herrick, *Tragicomedy: Its Origin and Development in Italy, France, and England* (Urbana, 1955), pp. 227–8.
26 *Rival Traditions*, p. 55

of the other plays is certainly found in the scenes depicting civic virtues in *If You Know Not Me*, but the treatment of the young prodigals in this play and in *The Wise-woman of Hogsdon* (c. 1604) is casual and even amoral in a way that is by no means characteristic (this point is considered more fully in chapter 3). Both comedies, though not unsophisticated, have a breezy, careless quality not found in the witty satires of the boys' companies or the firmly moral productions of the other adult troupes.

If there is little satire in most public theatre comedies, the deficiency is amply made up in the work of Ben Jonson, who wrote some plays for the child actors, but whose most important work was done for the adult companies. His satire is at once more powerful and more universal than that of the private theatres; it strikes through the cheats and follies of the playwright's age to the essential folly and knavery of man. His plays have both continental and English roots. As Madeleine Doran puts it, 'In the great comedies, the tightly managed intrigue and the outward shape of the plot are like Latin and Italian comedy; yet the motivation of the intrigue in satirically-conceived character, or rather in common human impulses of greed and folly, makes these plays fundamentally unlike Latin comedy. In their moral-psychological combination of motives they seem to me to have closer affinity with the morality play tradition. But essentially they are something new, a distinct form in themselves.'[27]

It is possible that Jonson revised *Every Man in his Humour* (Chamberlain's, 1598) around 1605,[28] and that his decision to turn his first major play into a thoroughgoing London comedy was influenced by the success of *Westward Ho* and its sequels.[29] In any case, by 1610, in the prologue to *The Alchemist* (King's), we find him firmly committed to the London setting and the depiction of native, contemporary follies. His commitment came later than that of Dekker or Middleton; but unlike those dramatists he was to keep to it consistently in the years ahead. After *Bartholmew Fair* (Lady Elizabeth's, 1614) his work becomes, on the surface, more strictly topical, but he clings to his essential purposes in comedy while other writers shift and change.

After 1610, the development of citizen comedy becomes increasingly blurred and confused. The concentrated movements of the first decade begin to peter out, and with the adult companies moving into the private theatres it becomes less meaningful to draw distinctions between public and private repertories. It also becomes more difficult to identify plays as unquestionably citizen comedies. Few of them focus clearly on the middle class; genres also become more

27 *Endeavors of Art* (Madison, 1954), p. 169
28 See Chambers, *Elizabethan Stage*, III, 360; and Henry Holland Carter, Introduction to his edition of the play (New Haven, 1921), pp. lviii–lxviii.
29 See Felix E. Schelling, *Elizabethan Drama 1558–1642* (New York, 1959), I, 529.

mixed, and comedy co-exists with romance and melodrama in many cases. In older plays of the public theatres, we found comedy pushed towards domestic tragedy; in these later plays, it is more a case of two genres existing side by side in a single play. Many plays in this group are written by various combinations of Middleton, Rowley, and Webster: *A Fair Quarrel* (Prince's, *c.* 1617) and *Anything for a Quiet Life* (King's, *c.* 1621) are typical cases. They are characterized, on the whole, by an interest in intrigue and superficially effective situations, to which all else is sacrificed; and by a certain sentimentality and lack of moral grip.[30] A wide range of social classes is depicted, but interest tends to centre on ladies and gentlemen rather than citizens. Some of the social themes dealt with earlier in the private theatres (usury and social climbing, for example) recur, but the old satiric vigour is gone.

Among the more attractive (and certainly the more single-minded) productions of this period are the comedies of John Fletcher. He takes plot materials from both the private and public traditions, softening the satire of the one and draining away the morality of the other. The emphasis is on entertainment, provided by witty dialogue, clever intrigue, and an overall air of playful fantasy. Like other playwrights of the period, he concentrates on the gentry. In such plays as Massinger's *A New Way to Pay Old Debts* (Red Bull Company? later, Queen Henrietta's, 1621) and Davenport's *A New Trick to Cheat the Devil* (Queen Henrietta's? *c.* 1625) there is something like the shrewd commentary on men and society we found in the best of the earlier comedies. But in general the elements of citizen comedy that seem to have the greatest power of survival after 1610 are the London setting, the intrigue, and the interest in one particular class, the idle young men about town. These are the chief debts that Caroline and Restoration comic writers owe to their Jacobean forbears. But the keen, critical judgment of men in society that distinguishes the best work of Jonson, Middleton, and Dekker, was never quite recovered.

30 See Elmer Edgar Stoll, *John Webster: the Periods of his Work Determined by his relations to the Drama of his Day* (Boston, 1905), p. 191.

2
Citizen hero and citizen villain

'And money is like muck, not good except it be spread.'
Francis Bacon, 'Of Seditions and Troubles'

The Elizabethans, faced with the vigorous expansion of commercial life in their time, and contemplating the often spectacular careers of capitalists and entrepreneurs, were not always sure that they approved. They had inherited a firm tradition of Christian disapproval of covetousness, 'the foulest fiend and blackest devil of all the rest,' which 'murdereth our merchants, [and] stingeth our mariners.'[1] Puritan divines like Arthur Dent, the author of those words, attacked the unseemly eagerness to make money as part of the general decadence of the times. But it is understandable that such criticism constituted only one part of the public response to what Ben Jonson called 'the money-get, mechanic age.'[2] Money is not just the root of all evil: it is a source of real power, and – especially to those who do not have much of it and do not fully understand how it works – it often looks like magic. There is in the popular literature of the time a vein of unabashed excitement in the power of wealth. In the prose fiction of Thomas Deloney, which appears to be aimed at middle-class readers, the rise of the citizen hero is proudly celebrated. In his *Jack of Newberry* (1597) we are shown Jack's progress from apprentice to master of his household, employer of hundreds of happy workers, a man who can equip a large company of soldiers and stage a sumptuous banquet for the king. The story reads like

---

1 Arthur Dent, *The Plaine Mans Path-way to Heauen* ... (London, 1607), pp. 66, 71. On the pamphlet campaign against the new commercialism, see L.C. Knights, *Drama and Society in the Age of Jonson* (Harmondsworth, 1962), pp. 119–41.
2 'An Expostulation with Inigo Jones,' l.52

a fantasy of wish-fulfilment, and for most of its readers it probably was; but it was not without its basis in reality. For a London tradesman, there was a clearly established ladder of promotion – apprentice, independent businessman, sheriff, alderman, and finally Lord Mayor, a position of considerable honour and importance. It was right and proper to try to climb this ladder;[3] and every year there was a new Lord Mayor.

But the celebration of the wealthy citizen hero in popular literature often mixes more sober social considerations with the glamour. Francis Bacon's dictum that 'Riches are for spending, and spending for honour and good actions'[4] proclaims a somewhat aristocratic ideal of the responsibilities of a great man, but it was an ideal the mercantile classes evidently liked to think they could emulate. John Stow records in his *Survey of London* (1598) a long list of public works performed by citizens – the founding of hospitals, prisons, and colleges, the supplying of corn during famine, legacies for the poor, and so forth – philanthropy on a colossal scale.[5] The fascination with the power of wealth is clear enough, but there is also an insistence that power should be directed to worthy social ends, that a great fortune is not a private blessing but a public trust.

What concerns us, however, is the celebration of the wealth and social usefulness of the citizen-hero as we find it in the theatre, for it is a small but conspicuous part of the range of plays I have chosen to call citizen comedy. For the dramatist, the material of civic legends offers many opportunities, and some problems. It is a way to easy popularity with at least one section of the public; it allows a central figure who can easily win over the audience through rousing speeches and touching acts of generosity. But the gradual accumulation of wealth, venture by venture and year by year, which the writer of fiction or chronicle can summarize readily, is intractable material for the dramatist: the pace is wrong. The single figure dispensing bounty is a static concept for a medium that thrives on showing the complex interactions of a man with his fellows. Also, the dramatist has less direct control over his audience's responses than the non-dramatic writer. The latter can pause, analyse, explain, and if necessary apologize; he has all the time he wants to take. But the dramatist has only two or three hours, and no chance to interrupt the performance. He must *show* us, not tell us, and leave us to respond in the way the material dictates; or, if he is to guide us, his means of doing so must be economical. And in the story of the citizen hero some guiding may be necessary, for the display of wealth can look like mere ostentation, and the climb up the social ladder, excit-

---

3 See Anthony Nixon, *A Straunge Foot-Post ...* (London, 1613), sigs. E⁴v-F¹r; and Knights, *Drama and Society*, p. 27.
4 'Of Expense,' in *Essays*, ed. F.G. Selby (London, 1889, repr. 1958), p. 73
5 Henry Morley, ed. (London, 1890), pp. 130–1

ing though it may be to some members of the audience, may look like vulgar pushiness to others. Francis Lenton describes 'a peremptory citizen ... who, not long since, descended from the loins of some lubbardly farmer, and is now by giddy fortune furred all over, and in the vanity of his spirit looks askance if you miss the title of Master Alderman.'[6] Not everyone succumbed to the charm of the Dick Whittington legend.

A simple approach to some of these problems can be seen in William Rowley's *A New Wonder, a Woman Never Vexed* (auspices unknown, *c* 1625). Here the virtues of the exemplary citizen are displayed by contrast with a less worthy example of the class. The play as a whole is an elaborate exploration of the theme of charity, public and private. Private charity is treated in the story of the prodigal Stephen Foster, who will be discussed in the next chapter; public charity finds its expression in the good works of the merchant Brewen, who builds a hospital, and of Stephen who, recalling his misery when he was imprisoned for debt, remodels Ludgate on more attractive lines. The problem of the dramatic presentation of public works projects will appear later in a discussion of Heywood's *If You Know Not Me, You Know Nobody, Part Two*, which this part of Rowley's play seems to be imitating. I am concerned now with a more effective scene, contrasting Brewen and Old Foster, the good merchant and the bad.

They have combined on a trading venture which seems about to give them a handsome profit. As the news comes that the ships are on their way, Brewen immediately begins to plan his hospital, while Old Foster dreams of personal pomp, and of rising, not safely within his class, but vaingloriously out of it:

OLD FOSTER ...titles will faster come,
Than we shall wish to have them.
BREWEN Faith, I desire none. (III.i.p.145)

Brewen modestly refuses to parade his wealth, while Old Foster glories in public display:

Would they were cover'd, George; 'tis too public
Blazon of my estate. (III.i.p.153)
Listen their arrival, and bid the gunner speak it
In his loud thunder all the city over;
Tingle the merchants' ears with the report
Of my abundant wealth. (III.i.p.154)

6 *Characterismi* (London, 1631), sigs. D⁵r-v

Old Foster's punishment for his pride in wealth is appropriate: in his desire to gain more, he overreaches himself, and loses everything. Thinking to make an extra gain, he buys Brewen's share of the venture from him before the fleet actually arrives, giving Brewen all his present goods in lieu of payment. The fleet then sinks, leaving Foster with nothing. Brewen's wealth, about which he was humble and self-effacing, is used for the permanent good of society; Old Foster's fortune, about which he was unduly proud, simply disappears.

In this scene the business of money-making is neatly reduced to a single dramatic episode, showing one critical event. And our approval of Brewen is clinched by the portrayal of Old Foster, who so obviously displays the wrong attitude that any possible criticism of his colleague is deflected. Moreover, it is worth noting that the test on the characters (for that is what the scene provides) is essentially a test of *attitude*, not of action. Old Foster does nothing illegal or even unethical. He is a member of a perfectly respectable profession, and there is nothing dishonourable about the way he accumulates wealth. But he is proud and self-centred, and this is his offence in terms of the simple moral diagram on which the scene is based.

This scene serves to introduce what is perhaps the major consideration in the dramatization of wealth, its uses and abuses, in citizen comedy. If the rich citizen were self-absorbed and egotistic in his use of wealth, he would be a proper object for satire – particularly in view of comedy's traditional hostility to the crabbed and egocentric. But if he is socially outgoing, the medium of dramatic comedy should show him at his best; and there is always the opportunity to build on the abstract idea of generosity a lively and attractive personality, if the dramatist cares to seize the chance. This is precisely what Thomas Dekker does in *The Shoemakers' Holiday* (Admiral's, 1599). Simon Eyre, the shoemaker who rises to be Lord Mayor of London, enlivens the middle-class virtue of hard work with a remarkably salty tongue:

Where be these boys, these girls, these drabs, these scoundrels, they wallow in the fat brewis of my bounty, and lick up the crumbs of my table, yet will not rise to see my walks cleansed; come out you powder-beef-queans, what Nan, what Madge Mumble-crust, come out you fat midriff-swag-belly whores, and sweep me these kennels, that noisome stench offend not the nose of my neighbours; what Firk I say, what Hodge! Open my shop windows, what Firk I say. (1.iv.1-8)

The comic fantasy of the speech, with its headlong pace and its genial insults, springs initially from the working-day world, from Eyre's shop and occupation. Throughout the play, the shoemaker moves in a constant whirl of activity, issuing orders left and right. There are few plays in which the ordinary business of plying a craft is so successfully dramatized, and (while Dekker sometimes shows the men at work on stage) much of the effect is achieved by the sheer energy of Eyre's language. This is one solution to the problem of making trade dramatic.

But Eyre's success as a shoemaker is not directly responsible for his advancement; and here Dekker's material presents him with problems, with which he deals adroitly. The play is not as ingenuous as it may appear: Dekker is well aware of the kind of criticism that can be levelled at his hero, and quietly forestalls it. Eyre makes his fortune by a commercial venture, buying a cargo of merchandise from a Dutch skipper, which he is able to resell at a handsome profit to himself. Dekker is at pains to assure us that Eyre is not cheating the skipper, for the transaction takes place on the latter's own suggestion (II,iii.13–18). The affair is curiously underplayed: the relevant action takes place offstage, and we are given only the most meagre details about it. Dekker's departure from his source here is significant, for it involves the (I think) deliberate suppression of material. In Deloney's *The Gentle Craft*, to which Dekker is largely indebted, Eyre indulges in a bit of subterfuge in order to get his hands on the cargo before paying for it; he even disguises himself in the process. He is urged on by his wife, who is presented, quite frankly, as covetous.[7] The only trace of any of this that survives in Dekker's play is the scene in which Eyre dons an alderman's gown before going to see the skipper (II.iii.94–114).[8] But there is no hint in the play that the gown is in any way a disguise, or that it has not been come by honestly. Its only dramatic function is to signal the start of Eyre's rise to eminence. Dekker, in order to show Eyre as an example to proper social behaviour, is more careful than Deloney to keep his hero, in the eyes of the audience, innocent of greed or guile.

Dekker is also careful to free the shoemaker from any taint of ambition in connection with his advancement in the world. Promotion, like his fortune, simply comes his way, and he welcomes it casually:

LORD MAYOR ... Master Eyre, I hope ere noon to call you Sheriff.
EYRE I would not care, my lord, if you might call me King of Spain; come, Master Scot. (III.i.82–4)

Even his elevation to Lord Mayor, when we first hear of it, is only mentioned in passing (IV.iii.14–16). Mistress Eyre, who lets promotion go to her head and

7 See *The Works of Thomas Deloney*, ed. F.O. Mann (Oxford, 1912), pp. 112–15.
8 See Marie-Thérèse Jones-Davies, *Un Peintre de la Vie Londonienne: Thomas Dekker* (Paris, 1958), I, 128.

starts dreaming of French hoods and farthingales, is the target of some genial satire (III.ii.32–6). In short, while Eyre attacks his new responsibilities with gusto, his actual rise to eminence is curiously played down. Dekker, I think, is aware that ambition and the profit motive should not touch his hero too closely. By a dramatic sleight-of-hand, he throws the shoemaker's shop into prominence, and distracts us from the real source of the hero's fortune. The impression that lingers in the memory, after a casual perusal of the play, is that Simon Eyre became Lord Mayor of London because he was a jolly and energetic shoemaker.

At the end of the play, the emphasis is on the benevolent use to which Eyre puts his fortune once he has it. This is something that Dekker can dramatize with confidence. In keeping with the robust temper of the comedy, the shoemaker's benevolence expresses itself not in great public buildings but in great public banquets. His building of Leadenhall is mentioned, but Dekker wisely concentrates on the feasts, since there is more fun to be had from them. The apprentices' banquet is such a good party that even the dishes seem to come to life and join in:

Oh Hodge, oh my brethren! There's cheer for the heavens, venison, pasties walk up and down piping hot, like sergeants, beef and brewis comes marching in dry fats, fritters and pancakes comes trolling in wheelbarrows, hens and oranges hopping in porters' baskets, collops and eggs in scuttles, and tarts and custards comes quavering in in malt shovels. (v.ii.188–94)

The generous man's reward is that his memory will live; and Eyre's memory lives in a particularly genial way, in the holiday from which the play takes its name:

Besides, I have procur'd, that upon every Shrove Tuesday, at the sound of the pancake bell, my fine dapper Assyrian lads shall clap up their shop windows, and away; this is the day, and this day they shall do't, they shall do't:
    Boys, that day you are free, let masters care,
    And prentices shall pray for Simon Eyre. (v.i.47–52)

The last line shows Eyre in the perspective of folk-tales and chronicles, as the hero of the Gentle Craft.

The play is, in fact, a dramatized folk-tale, a fantasy of success. What gives it its peculiar strength is that the fantasy is subtly but firmly linked to the realities of life. Eyre works in a real shop: the jobs to be done, and even the tools of the trade, are set forth in detail (1.iv.70–4). Eyre balks at hiring a new workman simply because the others find him a good fellow: 'Peace Firk, a hard world, let him pass, let him vanish, we have journeymen enow, peace my fine Firk' (I.iv.46–7). He does hire him in the end, because the workman is young Roland Lacy in disguise, and the romantic plot demands that he work for Simon Eyre; but the awareness of business realities – 'a hard world' – is there all the same, and it acts as a counterbalance to the fantasy. One of the play's songs hints that the world is not all sunshine and success:

Cold's the wind and wet's the rain,
    Saint Hugh be our good speed;
Ill is the weather that bringeth no gain,
    Nor helps good hearts in need. ('The Second Three-man's Song,' 1–4)

For the most part, the play projects the values of good business and good fellowship with an air of comic fantasy; but the song reminds us that prosperity must be linked with generosity, not only in the golden world of civic legends but in the world of hard reality as well.

In part, Dekker achieves his purpose by a series of rather crafty tactical retreats, deliberately limiting the scope of his play. He fleshes out the idea of public generosity in a single, richly conceived figure, who carries a good deal of ethical weight, but carries it lightly. It looks easy, but this appearance is deceptive. Just how deceptive it is can be seen when we compare Simon Eyre with the citizen heroes of Thomas Heywood's *If You Know Not Me, You Know Nobody, Part Two* (Queen Anne's 1605). Where Dekker is controlled, Heywood is expansive, casting about for a variety of ways to display citizen virtue. Old Hobson, one of the play's leading merchants, appears to be Heywood's attempt to create a citizen who, like Eyre, is jovial in demeanour and exemplary in conduct. He comes breezing into his shop:

Where be these varlets? Bones a' me, at tavern?
Knaves, villains, spend-goods; foot, my customers
Must either serve themselves, or pack unserved. (p. 257)

But putting this beside Eyre's speech rousing his household, we see that the pungency of language is missing: Heywood lacks Dekker's imaginative freedom with words. Throughout the play, Heywood tries to give Hobson 'character' by having him exclaim 'Bones a' me!' at regular intervals, but this is no substitute for real verbal inventiveness. And with his jolliness goes a childlike naïveté, as when a representative of the crown comes to him for a routine loan:

How! Bones a' me, Queen know Hobson, Queen know Hobson?
And send for but one hundred pound? Friend, come in;
Come in, friend, shall have two; Queen shall have two. (p. 287)

Later, he is bewildered when the Queen does not recognize him (pp. 317–18).
It was always possible to believe in Eyre as a shrewd man of the world beneath
his flamboyance; but Hobson is a figure of pure fantasy, and when, in the later
scenes, he becomes a jolly rich uncle scattering bounty among the London poor
(pp. 319–20), it is all stage money, and the effect is of pleasant wish-fulfilment,
and nothing more.

But the crucial scenes are Heywood's depiction of the career of Thomas
Gresham, with his building of the Royal Exchange. (On the title page of the
first edition, in 1606, this is mentioned just after the main title, in large type;
the play's other main historical event, the defeat of the Armada, brings up the
rear, in smaller type.) Gresham is the prototype of business virtue, the man
who makes his money honestly and uses it for the common good. The range
of values that Heywood tries to embody in this figure is considerably wider than
we find in *The Shoemakers' Holiday*, and the dramatization of civic virtue is
consequently more elaborate. It includes patriotism (touched on only briefly by
Dekker): the building of the Royal Exchange is viewed as a matter of civic and
national pride, and the point is rammed home in a scene in which two much-
travelled lords compare the Exchange favourably with what they have seen in
Constantinople, Rome, Venice, and Antwerp (pp. 295–6). When Gresham is
praised for embarking on a venture in Barbary sugar which the best merchants
of France and Spain had been too timid to risk, he is praised as a patriot: 'Tis
held your credit and your country's honour' (p. 253). Religion is also invoked.
Gresham adopts the traditional, pious attitude that he is 'by God's blessing only
raised' (p. 278), and the preacher Dr Nowell, urging Gresham to follow the
example of public charity set by great men of the past, sees it in religious as
well as social terms: 'If you will follow the religious path / That these have beat
before you, you shall win Heaven' (p. 278). The chief emphasis, however, is
on the permanent credit such public works give to the founder. Gresham, seeing
Nowell's portrait gallery of public benefactors, remarks,

And we may be ashamed,
For in their deeds we see our own disgrace.
We that are citizens, are rich as they were,
Behold their charity in every street,
Churches for prayer, alms-houses for the poor,

Conduits which bring us water; all which good
We do see, and are reliev'd withal,
And yet we live like beasts, spend time and die,
Leaving no good to be remember'd by. (p. 277)

This speech is the measure of the difference between Heywood's play and
Dekker's. Heywood is more discursive, more explicit; he spells out ideas that
are implicit in the earlier play. The scene in Nowell's portrait gallery is an illustrated lecture on public charity, and throughout the play even the most obvious
actions are not allowed to speak for themselves. When, for example, to show
his indifference to a loss he has suffered, Gresham powders a valuable pearl and
drinks it, his fellow merchant Ramsey calls our attention to his virtues, and
Gresham carefully explains his own motives:

RAMSEY
You are an honour to all English merchants;
As bountiful as rich, as charitable
As rich, as renowned as any of all.
GRESHAM
I do not this as prodigal of my wealth;
Rather to show how I esteem that loss
Which cannot be regain'd. (p. 301)

In particular, the Royal Exchange scenes suffer from this overexplicitness. The
erection of a building is not an obvious subject for drama, and the detailed expla-
nations of such matters as storage and ventilation, though designed to make
Gresham's care more evident, and the building itself more vivid to the audience,
are not what one could call compelling theatre.

Gresham, like Eyre, is a legendary folk-hero; but the element of fantasy in
his presentation, like the moralizing, gets out of control, as it does in the character of Hobson. In return for his Barbary sugar venture – a risk of sixty thousand
pounds – Gresham gets only a pair of slippers and a dagger. This is how he
reacts:

What, sixty thousand pound in sterling money,
And paid me all in slippers? Then hoboys, play!
On slippers I'll dance all my care away.
...
You may report, lords, when you come to Court,

You Gresham saw a pair of slippers wear,
Cost thirty thousand pound. (pp. 300–1)

This is fantasy, and has to be taken as such; but it lacks the ballast of reality
that made Dekker's fantasy more easily acceptable. Gresham seems, at
moments like this, to be a creature of a totally unreal world. Not that the play
lacks a sense of reality elsewhere; there are several scenes which show the day-
to-day business of buying and selling in a concrete, convincing way – 'Come,
fellow Crack, have you sorted up those wares? / Mark'd them with 54? They
must be pack'd up' (p. 283). But fantasy and reality remain in separate compart-
ments, and never fuse – as they do in *The Shoemakers' Holiday* – into a coherent whole.

There is, in Heywood's portrayal of commercial life, a slightly defensive
attitude, and I think this is connected with the play's dramatic weaknesses.
Heywood seems excessively anxious to point out that prudence and business
acumen are not sins, and that the merchants he portrays are, despite their great
gains, neither cruel nor dishonest:

FACTOR
Neither to flatter, nor detract from him,
He is a merchant of good estimate:
Care how to get, and forecast to increase,
(If so they be accounted) be his faults.
MERCHANT
They are especial virtues, being clear
From avarice and base extortion. (p. 251)

Heywood seems to be expecting an unfriendly voice at the back of the theatre,
which must be silenced. The damage is twofold: the propaganda is less effective
because it protests too much, and seems to lack the courage of its convictions;
and the drama suffers through being cluttered with unnecessary explanation
and analysis. The dramatization of citizen virtue is flamboyant but fundamentally uncertain; beside this play *The Shoemakers' Holiday*, for all its breezy
good temper, is revealed as a controlled work of art.

In all these plays the inherent values are conventional, and what concerns
us is the dramatic life with which those values are clothed. The dramatists'
major advantage, one which Dekker uses most effectively, is that social generosity is a value for which comedy has a natural sympathy. The traditional
happy ending of comedy – the feast or celebration – is easy to link with the figure

of the philanthropic citizen hero. Conversely, any comedy which involves money (and this includes most citizen comedies) and which needs a villain can easily create one in the figure of the close-fisted miser. As Northrop Frye has pointed out, the basic intrigue pattern of New Comedy demands, usually, an interfering old man, who stands in the way of the hero's pursuit of money, or a girl, or both, and who must be defeated to ensure the happy ending.[9]

The character who fills this function in numerous citizen comedies is the usurer. Basically, his role is structural: he is an impediment to be overcome. But for the audience to enjoy his discomfiture fully, a certain amount of hostility must be created towards him, and it appears that in the case of the usurer this hostility was ready-made. Usury was attacked in pamphlet after pamphlet, and the usurer – like the villainous landlord of Victorian melodrama – seems to have been a popular bogeyman.[10] Dramatists in both the public and private theatres seized on the character as a handy device, and used it automatically, as a convenient symbol for all the life-denying forces which are opposed and finally swept away by the action of the comedy. He is always an old man, and this naturally leads to jokes about his impotence, which have a special symbolic value in plays in which he impedes a love affair. Obsessed with the barren breeding of gold,[11] he is a figure of sterility standing in the way of the renewal of life to which comedy strives. He is a citizen, in that he represents the mercantile classes, but he is a citizen villain, by the same standards that make the leading characters of Deloney, Dekker, and Heywood citizen heroes.

9 'The Argument of Comedy,' *English Institute Essays, 1948* (New York, 1949), p. 58
10 Thomas Lodge's description is typical: 'he is narrow-browed, and squirrel-eyed, and the chiefest ornament of his face is, that his nose sticks in the midst like an embossment in terrace work, here and there embellished and decked with *verucae* for want of purging with agaric; some authors have compared it to a rutter's codpiece, but I like not the allusion so well, by reason the tyings have no correspondence. His mouth is always mumbling, as if he were at his matins: and his beard is bristled here and there like a sow that had the lousy. Double-chinned he is, and over his throat hangs a bunch of skin like a money-bag. Bands wears he none, but a welt of coarse holland, and if you see it stitched with blue thread, it is no workaday wearing. His truss is the piece of an old packcloth, the mark washed out; and if you spy a pair of Bridges' satin sleeves to it, you may be assured it is a holiday ... Thus attired, he walks Paul's, coughing at every step as if he were broken-winded, grunting sometime for the pain of the stone and strangury: and continually thus old, and seeming ready to die, he notwithstanding lives to confound many families' – from *Wits Miserie* ... (1596), cited in *Life in Shakespeare's England*, ed. John Dover Wilson (Harmondsworth, 1959), pp. 158–60. For a general discussion of the attacks on usury, see Knights, *Drama and Society*, pp. 138–41.
11 Cf. Henry Smith, *The Examination of Usurie* (London, 1591): 'When God had finished his creation, he said unto man, and unto beasts, and unto fishes, increase and multiply, but he never said unto money, increase and multiply, because it is a dead thing, which hath no seed, and therefore is not fit to engender' (pp. 16–17).

In particular, he opposes the spirit of feasting and celebration embodied in characters like Eyre. Hoarding his money instead of spending it, he denies joys to others, and to himself. In Marston's *Jack Drum's Entertainment* (Paul's, c. 1600) the usurer Mammon rebukes the genial knight Sir Edward Fortune for keeping too great a house – in other words, for practising the old-fashioned virtue of hospitality – and is rebuked in turn by Sir Edward's reply, 'tush, tush, your life hath lost his taste' (i.i.p.183). Pennyboy senior, in Jonson's *The Staple of News* (King's, 1626), is sent lavish gifts of food, which he is quite unable to enjoy:

Yonder is venison sent me! fowl! and fish!
In such abundance! I am sick to see it!
I wonder what they mean! I ha' told 'em of it!
To burthen a weak stomach! and provoke
A dying appetite! (ii.iii.25–9)

The usurer's love of money deadens his capacity for ordinary enjoyment, and makes him the natural opponent of the livelier characters in the play, just as his impotence makes him the natural opponent of love-matches.

Accordingly, he is fair game for the roughest treatment. He is made the butt of the others characters' jokes – sometimes quite savage jokes, as in *The Honest Lawyer* by 'S.S.' (Queen Anne's, c. 1615), in which Valentine, pretending to cure the usurer Gripe of gout, drives a nail through his foot. He suffers defeat in the love-intrigue, being cheated of the woman he wants to marry, as in *Jack Drum's Entertainment* and William Rowley's *A Match at Midnight* (Red Bull, c. 1622), or of the match he wants for his daughter, as in William Haughton's *Englishmen for my Money* (Admiral's, 1598) and the anonymous *Wily Beguiled* (Paul's? c. 1602). The most significant punishment, of course, is the loss of his money. We see here the conventional idea that a fortune ill-got and selfishly used can have no permanence.[12] The thieves who, disguised as fairies, rob Gripe in *The Honest Lawyer*, make it clear that he is being punished for failing to use his riches charitably:

Whiles thy house was cleanly swept,
And thy conscience chastely kept;

12 Cf. W.M., *The man in the moone … or the English Fortune-teller* (London, 1609): 'Nay, thy wife shall be enamoured of some spend-all, which shall waste all as licentiously as thou hast heaped together laboriously; thy children never thrive with aught thou didst bequeath them, it was so vilely gotten, and thy name either utterly blotted out, or remain infamous to posterity.' (sig.E1v).

Neat linen, fire and water ready;
And thy purpose good and steady;
Whiles thou never sent the poor
Unrewarded from thy door,

...

We brought thee wealth, but 'twas in vain;
For now we'll fetch it back again. (sigs. G²v-³r)

Hog, in Robert Tailor's *The Hog hath Lost his Pearl* (privately acted at White-friars, 1613) is deluded by a false vision of Croesus, during which his treasure is spirited away; the mock-religious tone of the vision indicates that Hog is being punished for his idolatrous worship of gold.[13] The usurer's distorted values form the basis for another standard punishment: being an unbalanced character to begin with, he sometimes runs completely mad at the loss of his gold. Mammon has an extravagant tirade of despair; Pennyboy senior berates a porter for having spent sixpence, and ends by putting his two dogs on trial. In the end, the usurer may repent and reform, but such repentances are usually perfunctory; there is more dramatic vitality in the punishments that produce them. We do not feel, as we do with the prodigal, the usurer's opposite number, that penitence is the *raison d'être* of the punishment; rather, the punishment exists in its own right. The usurer is not a lost sheep to be recovered, but an enemy to be overcome.[14]

Naturally, as there is little variation in his dramatic function, one stage usurer is very much like another; he has the automatism and predictability of any traditional comic butt.[15] This probably extended to a standardized,

---

13 We are made to feel that, since usury is simply legalized theft, there is nothing unethical in robbing a usurer; it is simply tit for tat. Vaster, one of the thieves in *The Honest Lawyer*, and a former victim of Gripe, makes this point:

Is't sin to rob the thief? By usurious course,
He once robb'd me, now I rob him by force.
No difference but this, 'twixt him and me –
I ha' not such protection, as had he. (sig. D²r)

14 An interesting exception is *Wily Beguiled*, in which the usurer's conversion (rising from his love for his daughter, who has made a love-match against his wishes) involves a fully dramatised choice between human and mercenary values. It is crudely done, but it is refreshing to see it done at all.

15 For a detailed and valuable survey of the usurer's stock characteristics, see Celeste Turner Wright, 'Some Conventions Regarding the Usurer in Elizabethan Literature,' *SP*, xxxi (April 1934), 176–97.

grotesque physical appearance. The cast-list of *Jack Drum's Entertainment* specifies 'Mammon the usurer, with a great nose' (p. 241), and Pisaro in *Englishmen for my Money* is described as having a 'snout, / Able to shadow Paul's, it is so great' (ll. 250–1). The standard anti-Semitic joke is probably implied here, since usury was regarded as a specialty of the Jews. His greed is always comically exaggerated, especially with reference to his interest rates. Mammon takes thirty in the hundred, while Algripe in Fletcher's *The Night Walker* (Lady Elizabeth's? c. 1611) and Bloodhound in *A Match at Midnight* take forty. Pisaro's twenty-two may seem mild by comparison, but we must remember that the maximum legal rate was ten per cent. [16]

In most of these cases, the dramatist does not bother to examine the reasons for the popular resentment of usury, accepting it simply as a convenient bond of sympathy between the audience and the leading characters. But Jonson's *The Staple of News* is an exception. The plot within which Pennyboy senior functions is not a conventional romantic intrigue but an elaborate exploration of the use and misuse of money, expressed allegorically through the various characters' relations with Lady Pecunia. The dramatic weight is thrown, not on the defeat of the usurer, but on the reasons why he is wrong: the prejudice is not merely used, but examined and explained. As Pecunia's guardian, Pennyboy senior keeps her too tightly locked up, and she chafes under the restraint, complaining that she needs air and exercise (ii.i.45–54). Instead of using her properly, he prostitutes her by lending her to his prodigal nephew. As Pennyboy Canter, the play's moral commentator, remarks, 'I see / A money-bawd is lightly a flesh-bawd too' (ii.v.99–100). The usurer debases money the way a bawd debases sex; and we recall the classic objections to making money engender. [17] The basic point that Jonson makes is that money should be neither hoarded nor abused. Pennyboy Canter lectures the usurer at the end of the play, advising him

To use her like a friend, not like a slave,
Or like an idol. Superstition
Doth violate the deity it worships,

16 See R.H. Tawney, *Religion and the Rise of Capitalism* (Harmondsworth, 1961), pp. 183–4.
17 On the connection between money and sex in this play, see Edward B. Partridge, *The Broken Compass* (London, 1958), p. 184. Usury is often described in sexual terms in contemporary writing, suggesting that it is not just an economic offence but an offence against nature: interest is 'the usurer's bastard,' and a broker who finds customers for a usurer is 'a pander.' See, respectively, Thomas Middleton, 'The Black Book,' in *The Works of Thomas Middleton*, ed. A.H. Bullen (London, 1885–6), viii, 18; and Barnaby Rich, *Favltes Favlts, and nothing else but Favltes* (London, 1606), sig.D¹v. Cf. also n.11, above.

No less than scorn doth. And believe it, brother,
The use of things is all, and not the store. (v.vi.22–6)

Pennyboy senior has made Pecunia both an idol and a slave; in his greed he
has worshipped her, and in his making of loans he has given her over to base
uses. Jonson has dramatized the objections to usury more fully than is customary, and the complaints of Pecunia herself at being shut up in a dark house give
a certain human, emotional colouring to an abstract idea, but the allegorical
machinery grinds too loudly for most tastes: Jonson, like Heywood in his very
different way, has fallen into the trap of being overexplicit.

Philip Massinger, on the other hand, succeeds as Dekker succeeds, by creating a vivid stage personality to embody the conventional social attitudes; the
difference is between a play that uses the natural resources of drama and one
that strains against them. Sir Giles Overreach in *A New Way to Pay Old Debts*
(Red Bull Company? 1621) has the same structural function as the stereotyped
stage usurer. He is the heavy father blocking his daughter's love-match
(whereas Simon Eyre encourages the love-match of Lacy and Rose), and the
financial villain who must be defeated if the hero is to recover his estate. But
the anti-social, life-denying qualities that he represents have more than a simple structural interest for Massinger. He views them with real horror, and
dwells on them in depth and in detail to make the audience share that horror.
Overreach is drawn on a much grander scale than the conventional stage usurer.
Usury, extortion, and the picking of legal quarrels are among his sources of
wealth; and there is a feeling throughout the play that we are seeing only a small
part of his power at work. There are continual hints of other ventures, which
are not made explicit, but kept as a vague, sinister background to the main
intrigue. And, while the stock usurer merely accumulates and hoards money,
Overreach is obsessed with power and the trappings of power. Instead of the
citizen hero's festive sharing of his wealth, we are shown a bloated and self-
centred extravagance:

And let no plate be seen, but what's pure gold,
Or such whose workmanship exceeds the matter
That it is made of ... (iii.ii.4–6)

Everything he does has to be done on a grand scale. He must not merely exploit
enough people to make him rich; he must exploit everyone: 'I must have all
men sellers, / And I the only purchaser' (ii.i.32–3). Greed has intensified into
megalomania, and the megalomania leads to violence. A certain Master Frugal
has the misfortune to own a piece of land that lies in the middle of Overreach's
estates:

I'll therefore buy some cottage near his manor,
Which done, I'll make my men break ope his fences;
Ride o'er his standing corn, and in the night
Set fire on his barns; or break his cattle's legs.
These trespasses draw on suits, and suits expenses,
Which I can spare, but will soon beggar him.
...
Then with the favour of my man of law,
I will pretend some title: want will force him
To put it to arbitrement: then if he sell
For half the value, he shall have ready money,
And I possess his land. (II.i.34–48)

The stereotyped stage usurer is also greedy for land, but he is interested in mere possession, more than in the social distinction that land implies.[18] Overreach's acquisition of land, however, is part of his campaign to crash into the upper classes. While the citizen-hero rises within his own class, keeping to the rules and harming no one, Overreach – the citizen villain – tries to rise out of his class, spreading hardship and misery as he does so. In the play, his possession of land is a *fait accompli* and he is now at work on a system of alliances. He himself had married Wellborn's aunt, and one of his chief projects now is the marriage of his daughter Margaret to Lord Lovell; he looks forward to calling her 'right honourable,' an expression that recurs obsessively in his speeches. He is almost servile in his politeness to Lovell; at the same time, he delights in humbling decayed aristocrats who are in his power:

'Tis a rich man's pride, there having ever been
More than a feud, a strange antipathy
Between us, and true gentry. (II.i.87–9)

He is, in fact, jealous of nobility, the one thing he cannot get by bullying, cheating, or bribery, and which he can enjoy only vicariously, through his daughter's marriage.[19]

His egotism is such that he does not even bother to conceal his nature under

18 A typical instance is Morecraft in Beaumont and Fletcher's *The Scornful Lady* (Queen's Revels? c. 1613).

19 For a useful study of Massinger's presentation of the social disruption caused by a burgeoning middle class, in this play and *The City-Madam*, see Alan Gerald Gross, 'Social Change and Philip Massinger,' *SEL*, VII (Spring 1967), 329–42.

a conventional surface; the other characters simply have to take him as they find him. This is how he describes himself to Lovell:[20]

Nay, when my ears are pierc'd with widows' cries,
And undone orphans wash with tears my threshold;
I only think what 'tis to have my daughter
Right honourable; and 'tis a powerful charm
Makes me insensible of remorse, or pity,
Or the least sting of conscience. (iv.i.126–31)

He is so wrapped up in himself that he does not bother to consider the effect he may be having on his listener. Nobody's opinion matters but his own.

In the end, he is defeated and runs mad. So did Mammon and Pennyboy senior; but Massinger uses this madness far more purposefully than do Marston and Jonson. It is a final comment on Overreach, showing his nature and relations with the world reduced to their simplest terms, translated into images by his disordered brain. His egotism has now isolated him completely.[21] He is only dimly aware of the other characters on stage, and his first words are, 'Why, is not the whole world / Included in my self?' (v.i.355–6). He then sees himself as he used to be, facing the world alone, and overcoming it; the essential violence of his conflict with society comes to the surface in images of battle:

say there were a squadron
Of pikes, lin'd through with shot, when I am mounted,
Upon my injuries, shall I fear to charge 'em?
No: I'll through the battalia, and that routed,
                    (Flourishing his sword sheathed)[22]
I'll fall to execution. (v.i.357–61)

20 This passage, and others like it, are often seen as an outside view of Overreach, which it is incredible to find the character himself expressing. See, for example, T.A. Dunn, *Philip Massinger: The Man and the Playwright* (Edinburgh, 1957), p. 133. This is certainly a possible view, and my interpretation is only credible if Overreach is seen as an absolute monster of egotism; but I would argue that he is just that, and that his mind is abnormal long before he goes completely mad.
21 See Joseph T. McMullen, Jr., 'Madness and the Isolation of Characters in Elizabethan and Early Stuart Drama,' *SP*, xlviii (April 1951), 206–18.
22 The Quarto of 1633 reads 'flourishing his sword unsheathed,' and this reading is retained by T.W. Craik in the New Mermaid edition (London, 1964). Though otherwise I have followed Craik, I have retained the more customary reading here, since it is clearly what the lines that follow require.

But the realization of his defeat paralyses him. In his one brief flash of moral insight he sees it as retribution. The widows' cries and orphans' tears he scorned when talking to Lovell return to haunt him:

> Ha! I am feeble:
> Some undone widow sits upon mine arm,
> And takes away the use of't; and my sword
> Glu'd to my scabbard, with wrong'd orphans' tears,
> Will not be drawn. (v.i.361–5)

He then sees shapes – presumably the other characters on the stage, who have defeated him – whom he calls first hangmen come to take him to the Judgement Seat, and then furies 'with steel whips / To scourge my ulcerous soul' (v.i.368–9). But the egotism reasserts itself, and he defies all punishment, and all judgment:

> shall I then fall
> Ingloriously, and yield? no, spite of fate,
> I will be forc'd to hell like to myself,
> Though you were legions of accursed spirits,
> Thus would I fly among you. (v.i.369–73)

He falls to the ground in a fit, and the man who boasted of his complete self-sufficiency has to be carried off the stage.

The intrigue against Overreach provides Massinger with problems that he does not altogether solve, as I will suggest in chapter 4; but the character himself is a vivid creation. While the average stage usurer is cold, negative, and not, in the end, very formidable, Overreach is a positive, destructive force. He is a villain in a comedy, but he is not a comic villain. The diseased, obsessive individualism he displays is too monstrous for laughter, and his defeat produces a sharper sense of relief than one normally experiences at the end of a comic action.

The plays we have looked at so far show that the comic form can in itself be a useful instrument of social analysis. Comedy normally moves towards harmony and social integration at the end – a marriage, a public celebration, the restoration of lost property – and our interest is held throughout by the battle against the selfish, anti-social characters who get in the way of this ending. The social issue of the use and misuse of wealth fits neatly into this pattern – so neatly that the results are often automatic and predictable. But the issue is capable of deeper exploration in dramatic terms, as the work of Dekker and Massinger shows. And it is worth noting that II *If You Know Not Me* and *The Staple of News*, experimental and discursive plays, make their social points less effectively than *The Shoemakers' Holiday* and *A New Way to Pay Old Debts*, which use the coventional devices of comedy as vehicles for social analysis, and which are still compelling theatre.

3
The prodigal

'Dost think, because thou are virtuous, there shall be no more cakes and ale?'
Twelfth Night

One of the most popular comic plots of the period was the story of the prodigal.
The rake's progress is, of course, a perennial theme, particularly in the theatre
(one thinks of such temperance melodramas as *The Drunkard* and *Ten Nights
in a Bar-Room*): it allows an audience the heady spectacle of debauchery and
the edifying spectacle of repentance, all for the price of one ticket. It provided
Hogarth with the subject for his most famous series of prints, and it has a
remarkably long history in European drama. In the early sixteenth century, the
schoolmasters of the Low Countries, while realizing the necessity of instructing
the young in the forms and metres of Latin comedy, had to admit that the examples which survived were neither Christian nor moral, and that something more
edifying in content was wanted. Accordingly, they produced a kind of drama
that allowed them to have the best of both worlds. Taking the Christian parable
of the prodigal son, they expanded the 'riotous living' mentioned only briefly
in the original into whole scenes of cheating and debauchery, which allowed
the New Comedy material of the ancients to be brought in – dissolute young
men, bawds, parasites, and the like. The rioting, however, was seen from a new
perspective of sober Christian moralizing and the end of the comedy was not
the victory of the young scapegrace in the worldly intrigues of Plautus and Terence, but his defeat on those terms, followed by his repentance and forgiveness,

taken sometimes word for word from the parable.[1] There is a similar dramatic pattern in the progress of the morality-play hero from drink and women to repentance and grace. The prodigal in citizen comedy has, then, a long stage history behind him.

The implicit social morality of the story is consistent with the conventional attitude to wealth glanced at in chapter 2: the prodigal's use of his money is not generosity but senseless, self-indulgent waste. Like the usurer, he is an easy figure to treat in an automatic way, and plays that survive show certain plot conventions recurring in various combinations. The hero may be a country gentleman wasting his substance in the city; he may reject normal social ties, usually by deserting his wife or rejoicing at his father's death. He then retires to an outlaw world of drinking, dicing, and whoring, a world that preys on him and then leaves him helpless. Isolated from society and deserted by his flatterers, he wanders aimlessly; he may be reduced to theft or begging, and he generally spends some time in prison. But there are agents of salvation at work, balancing the agents of destruction, as in a morality play. A loyal servant tries to keep the hero on the path of rectitude, usually without success. The father, or elder brother, whose death the prodigal rejoiced at because of the money left him, is really alive, watching him in disguise and engineering a plot to bring him to his senses. The wife he deserted remains loyal, and intercedes to save him at the last minute. If he is unmarried, a rich widow may pay his debts, or even marry him.[2] As the hero repents, society moves to reclaim him, and the social bonds he broke are restored. Behind the obvious lessons about drink, gambling, and painted women lies a much deeper interest in the importance – and self-healing power – of the social contract.

A characteristic play of this type is *The London Prodigal* (King's, c. 1604), which belongs firmly to the public theatre tradition of serious, moralizing comedy. Flowerdale, the hero, displays much of the conventional anti-social behaviour: when he is arrested for debt on his wedding morning, and his father-in-law revokes the dowry, he turns against his wife Luce and orders her away from him: 'Go, get you gone to the greasy chuff your father, bring me your dowry, or never look on me' (III.iii.255–7). His parting words to her are, 'Why,

1 See Charles H. Herford, *Studies in the Literary Relations of England and Germany in the Sixteenth Century* (Cambridge, 1886), pp. 84–8, 149–64; and Marvin T. Herrick, *Tragicomedy: Its Origin and Development in Italy, France, and England* (Urbana, 1955), pp. 22, 37–46.
2 This is a device which appears to have had some basis in the social facts of the time. According to Lawrence Stone, *The Crisis of the Aristocracy 1558–1641* (Oxford, 1965), widows 'were regarded at the time as the natural salvation of the bankrupt' (p. 622). Stone mentions several cases of widows being used for just this purpose.

turn whore, that's a good trade, / And so perhaps I'll see thee now and then'
(III.iii.295–6). His father, describing his capacity for running into debt, stresses
the harm this habit does to others:

For all the day he humours up and down,
How he the next day might deceive his friend.
He thinks of nothing but the present time:
For one groat ready down, he'll pay a shilling,
But then the lender must needs stay for it. (III.ii.165–9)

His father is spying on him in disguise, in the traditional manner, in order to
test his behaviour. He punishes him by having him arrested for debt, but punishment is all he achieves, and the only effect on Flowerdale is to drive him to
despair and fresh crimes. The prodigal falls into beggary and theft, and is finally
arrested for the murder of Luce, who has disappeared. In fact, she has been following his fortunes in disguise, and it is she who saves him at the end of the
play. Her loyalty (all the more remarkable in that she did not want to marry
him in the first place) impresses him, and shames him into repentance. What
punishment failed to achieve is brought about by his wife's selfless devotion.

All this is quite conventional; but the conventions are humanized, and the
moral judgments inherent in the story are broadened, in a way that is rather
attractive. A bare account of the action would make Flowerdale seem a paste-
board villain, but the dramatist has the good sense not to leave him at that. His
first reaction to his father's death manages to avoid both callous joy at what he
will inherit, and affected sorrow: 'Nay, I cannot weep you extempore; marry,
some two or three days hence, I shall weep without any stintance. But I hope
he died in good memory' (I.i.180–3). This turns to anger when he reads the
will, in which his only legacies are false dice and ironic aphorisms about prodigality; but the initial impression is a good one. There is also something engaging about his more innocent prodigal excesses: 'How now? fie, sit in the open
room? Now, good Sir Lancelot, and my kind friend worshipful Master
Weathercock! What, at your pint? A quart, for shame!' (I.ii.110–13). And his
more serious rioting, though talked about, is never shown on the stage. There
is also some criticism of the money-dominated society that rejects the prodigal.
Luce's father forces her to marry Flowerdale for mercenary reasons; then, when
the prodigal's arrest for debt reveals him as penniless, the old man repudiates
the match he himself has made, and disinherits his daughter for remaining loyal
to her husband. Throughout the scene of the arrest (which is designed as a test
for him, as much as for Flowerdale) he behaves as badly as does the prodigal

himself. In the same scene, Luce appeals to Flowerdale's uncle (at whose suit he has been arrested) to set him free. In her plea the whole business of imprisonment for debt, by which a commercially minded society chastises those who have lost their money, is called into question:

Alas, what good or gain can you receive,
To imprison him that nothing hath to pay?
And where nought is, the king doth lose his due:
Oh, pity him, as God shall pity you. (III.iii.202–5)

Logically speaking, this does not diminish Flowerdale's own crimes; but the theatrical effect is partly to deflect criticism from him to other targets, and partly to create sympathy for him as a victim. The audience, then, is never so alienated from the hero as to lose interest in his salvation, and this means that the comic ending of repentance and restoration is acceptable for more than simply structural reasons.

The London Prodigal, like The Shoemakers' Holiday, is a play that makes its self-appointed task look easier than it is. The balance and comparative good temper of this play may be emphasized by looking at other, more severe works in the same public-theatre tradition. In these plays, the moral issue is reduced to a simple black-and-white contrast between a wastrel husband and a loyal wife, put through their paces in a mechanically patterned action. Matheo, in the second part of Dekker's The Honest Whore (Prince Henry's, c. 1605), displays a crass cynicism towards his wife Bellafront: 'A poor gentlewoman, sir, whom I make use of a'nights' (III.ii.86). This cynicism is translated into action: when his taste for gaming and fine clothes has left him out of pocket, he demands that his wife return to her old profession. Vaster, in The Honest Lawyer, by 'S.S.' (Queen Anne's, c. 1615), actually sells his wife to a bawd in order to recover his losses. Arthur in How a Man May Choose a Good Wife From a Bad (Worcester's, c. 1602) and Vallenger in The Fair Maid of Bristow (King's, c. 1604) not only desert their wives for courtesans, but plot to have them murdered. This absolute villainy is met with an equally absolute loyalty. Mistress Arthur, though tempted, steadfastly refuses to commit adultery; Vallenger's wife refuses even to blame her husband for his outlandish behaviour: 'Call him not wretch, he is wretched but by me' (IV.i.587). In the end, when he is about to be executed for murder, she offers to die in his place, after even his own father has refused to save him. Bellafront, when Matheo is in Bridewell, makes a similar offer. Her father Orlando challenges her loyalty:

Dost thou beg for him, thou precious man's meat, thou? Has he not beaten thee, kick't thee, trod on thee, and dost thou fawn on him like a spaniel? Has he not pawn'd thee to thy petticoat, sold thee to thy smock, made ye leap at a crust, yet would'st have me save him?

BELLAFRONT
Oh yes, good sir, women shall learn of me,
To love their husbands in greatest misery,
Then show him pity, or you wrack my self. (v.ii.463–70)

Though, as it turns out, he does not really mean it, there is an air of exasperated common sense in Orlando's question to which it is difficult not to respond; and Bellafront's reply – especially 'women shall learn of me' – is chilling in its self-conscious artifice. Yet it represents the norm of this play, and of others of its kind. Absolute vice is confronted with absolute virtue, the characters become machines to illustrate moral points, and it is all done with a coldness of temper that is finally self-defeating. It is impossible to care about the husband or understand the wife, except as components of a simple moral diagram, and when the happy ending comes it produces only the rather cool satisfaction of seeing a predictable pattern completed.[3]

The story of the prodigal looks, in the abstract, coherent and easy to handle: all the dramatist has to do is put the characters through their paces. But evidently it needs careful treatment if it is to be theatrically satisfying and not merely logical. The author of *The London Prodigal* softens the hero's offences, and thus gives a *raison d'être* for the happy ending that is dramatic as well as moral. Ben Jonson in *The Staple of News* (King's, 1626) takes the conventional story and rationalizes it – as he does with the stereotype of the usurer in the same play – to show *why* each stage of the action is necessary. His dramatic idiom is different: this is not melodrama but satire. There is no belabouring of virtuous, unresisting women; the prodigal's real victim is himself, and this makes him more a fool than a villain. Pennyboy junior is, in fact, a characteristic Jonsonian gull. When the play opens, he is eagerly awaiting his coming of age; as soon as his watch strikes the magic hour, the stage fills with haberdashers, barbers, tailors, and other minions, who deck him out in the full panoply of folly. He pays his bills without examining them, he listens with childlike credulity to the wild tales of the newsmongers, and when he finally gets an idea for using his money on a public project, it is the founding of a Canter's College.

---

3 These plays are very similar in temper to the popular moralizing pamphlets and ballads which also told cautionary tales of the downfall of prodigals. A characteristic ballad title is 'A Warning to all Lewd Livers, by the Example of a disobedient Child, who riotously wasted and consumed his Father's and Mother's goods, and also his own, among strumpets and other lewd Livers, and after died most miserably on a Dunghill.' See *Roxburgh Ballads*, ed. W. Chappell, Vol. III, pt.1 (Hertford, 1875), pp. 22–8.

Just as his usurer uncle abuses Lady Pecunia by keeping her too tightly guarded, the prodigal abuses her by scattering her favours too promiscuously; in one heavily allegorical scene, he makes her kiss everybody in the room.

His supposedly dead father, disguised as an old canting beggar, watches him to see how he will use Pecunia; the Canter's College is the last straw. The father throws off his disguise (a ragged beggar's cloak) and lectures his son:

> ... and dost thou prostitute,
> Scatter thy Mistress' favours, throw away
> Her bounties, as they were red-burning coals,
> Too hot for thee to handle, on such rascals,
> Who are the scum and excrements of men?
> If thou hadst sought out good and virtuous persons
> Of these professions, I had lov'd thee, and them. (IV.iv.130–6)

He then strides off with Pecunia, leaving his son nothing but the ragged beggar's cloak. The change of costume both summarizes and explains the prodigal's punishment in a neat, theatrical way: he is under-dressed because he was previously over-dressed.[4]

The logical connection between offence and punishment is clearer than in the average prodigal play, but not essentially different in kind. More unusual is the rationalization of the hero's repentance and restoration. The average prodigal play ends with the hero stating that he has reformed and will do better in the future; beyond this the playwright does not usually bother to go. Pennyboy junior, however, shows his reformation in a practical way, not just by abandoning the world of knaves in which he committed his follies, but by beating the knaves at their own game: he successfully foils a plot by the crooked lawyer Picklock to cheat both him and his father. He shows in this a new shrewdness and a new sense of responsibility towards his father, who, in his turn, is favourably impressed:

> Put off your rags, and be yourself again;
> This act of piety, and good affection,
> Hath partly reconcil'd me to you. (v.iii.22–4)

The audience's amusement is carefully controlled throughout. It springs from a recognition of the prodigal's follies at first, and his later restoration is signalled by the fact that he gets not merely the last word over his enemies, but the last laugh.

It is, of course, characteristic of Jonson to exercise careful intellectual com-

---

4 The significance of clothes in this play is discussed by Edward B. Partridge, 'The Symbolism of Clothes in Jonson's Last Plays,' *JEGP*, LVI (1957), 396–409.

mand even over situations that might have been expected to provoke stock responses. But the major fascination of these prodigal comedies is that the stock moral attitudes simply cannot be relied on. When the story is dramatized, all sorts of possibilities can be released, and only the most sternly moral plays are content to let us condemn prodigality absolutely. We have seen how *The London Prodigal* is strengthened by allowing a variety of responses to the hero, and there are other plays which develop these responses further, even to the point at which the prodigal is no longer the major target of criticism. Latent in the story, for example, is sympathy for the prodigal as a victim of other people's coldness. From one point of view, his fate can be seen as a criticism of a society so obsessed with money that anyone who mishandles it is virtually destroyed. We see this in William Rowley's *A New Wonder, a Woman Never Vexed* (auspices unknown, *c.* 1625) and Robert Davenport's *A New Trick to Cheat the Devil* (Queen Henrietta's? *c.* 1625). Stephen Foster, in Rowley's play, is foolish and irresponsible, and there is no attempt to play down this side of his character. But the most severe criticism is levelled at his mean-spirited brother and sister-in-law, who object to the way Stephen is using up money, and particularly to the way his nephew Robin (Old Foster's son by a previous marriage) is aiding him. Robin lectures his father:

You cannot make a separation, sir,
Betwixt the duty that belongs to me
And love unto my uncle: as well you may
Bid me [to] love my maker, and neglect
The creature which he hath bid me [to] love:
If man to man join not a love on earth,
They love not heaven, nor him that dwells above it;
Such is my duty; a strong correlative
Unto my uncle – why, he's half yourself. (I.i.p. 106)

The play's basic lesson is the importance of charity – and this cuts across the criticism of prodigality, making the niggardly relatives who reject the prodigal seem more culpable than the prodigal himself.[5]

5 Stephen is, like many prodigals, rescued by a woman – in this case, the Widow, the 'woman never vexed' of the play's title, who is worried by the fact that she has never in her life suffered any misfortunes. She marries Stephen and puts him in charge of her estate, in the hope that he will ruin her. But as soon as he becomes her husband he reforms and begins to manage her estate so efficiently that he increases it, and uses his wealth to become not merely a respectable citizen but a great public benefactor. This might perhaps be taken as a rebuke to his mean-spirited relatives, indicating that had he been entrusted with more responsibility he would have proved his worth. But I think one must be careful here: his reform seems to be primarily a comic plot device, designed to heap more unwished-for good luck on the unfortunate Widow, and I think it is wise not to take it too seriously.

In Davenport's play, Slightall is criticized in the usual way for his social irresponsibility, but the main criticism is directed against those who have made him what he is. Respectable society and the outlaw world are both at fault. He receives a shock when his betrothed, Anne Changeable, breaks off their engagement at the instigation of her mother, in the hope of a more glamorous match with a lord. This gives him a cynical attitude towards women in general, and he embarks on a career of prodigality during which he intends to debauch every woman he can find. However, the debauchery, when it does take place, seems to be on a fairly ordinary scale, and what is most prominent dramatically is the conspiracy of the Usurer, the Scrivener, and the wicked servant Geoffrey to feed on his prodigality and bring him to ruin. When he is finally reduced to poverty, he is once more seen as a victim, rejected by the meanness of respectable society:

I'll prove my kindred; kindred hath he none
That hath not in his purse to rank with them.
My kindred wasted, as I spent my means;
Want makes me a mere stranger. Then my friends;
There's no such name for him whom need compels
To such extremes as I am newly fallen:
Relief from them, such as in cakes of ice
To him whose nerves and arteries are shrunk up
By bitter winter's fury. (II.iii.pp. 221–2)

The fact is that in the simple 'cautionary tale' view of prodigality there is nothing required beyond the hero's punishment. Our desire to see him restored must depend on our awareness that there are higher values than financial good sense, charity being one. In this way, the very fact that the prodigal is a figure in a comedy, requiring a happy ending, can broaden the moral base of the presentation.

But there is in comedy a much more serious threat to the simple moral presentation of the prodigal story. With the exception of *The Staple of News* the plays we have looked at are comedies largely by virtue of the happy ending: there is laughter in them, but it is generally kept in other areas of the play, safely away from the prodigal story, which is treated in the spirit of domestic drama. However, behind the moral dramas of the continental schoolmasters lay the deeper, older tradition of Plautus and Terence, where a young wastrel can win the audience over by wit, charm, and high spirits, by the sheer panache with which he tweaks the noses of the respectable on his way to winning the pot of gold and the girl. Allow enough of that kind of laughter (as opposed to the morally directed laughter of Jonson) into the prodigal story, and the simple moral pattern becomes impossible to maintain. A careful playwright can achieve a balance: the author of *The London Prodigal* rations the prodigal's appeal judiciously, and Thomas Heywood, in *The Wise-woman of Hogsdon* (Queen Anne's, *c.* 1604) manages to keep some kind of moral judgment intact while allowing his hero an amoral charm. It is no mean feat, and worth examining.

Chartley is a young country gentleman who has deserted his fiancée Luce and run off to London, where he wastes his estate in gambling. Yet even when she complains of his conduct, the terms she uses make it seem more scatter-brained than vicious: 'Oh this wild-headed, wicked Chartley, whom nothing will tame! To this gallant was I, poor gentlewoman, betrothed, and the marriage day appointed; but he, out of a fantastic and giddy humour, before the time prefixed, posts up to London' (i.ii.pp. 290–1). Once in London, he is smitten with another woman (who, confusingly, is also called Luce) and determines to enjoy her. She insists on marriage. Chartley's impatience with the normal sanctions is of a piece with the rest of his irresponsible behaviour: it might have been presented with stern disapproval, but Heywood prefers to allow him a rather engaging rakishness: 'I could like this marriage well, if a man might change away his wife still as he is aweary of her, and cope her away like a bad commodity; if every new moon a man might have a new wife, that's every year a dozen. But this 'till death us do part' is tedious (iii.i.p. 314). He is clearly a harebrained young man, but his actions seem to be the result of thoughtless whim rather than inherent viciousness.

This balanced attitude is reflected in Chartley's final correction. He is put in his place, but with indulgent laughter. He is placed in a room with several doors, in the Wise-woman's house, and there he is confronted with his misdeeds. He tries by falsehood to shift the blame onto other characters, but as he does so each person he accuses, in turn, steps into the room and denies the charge. The pattern is built up with comic inevitability, and Chartley's growing exasperation is a wonderfully amusing substitute for the conventional remorse.

We realize how neatly Heywood has struck the balance between judgment and indulgent laughter when we compare his play with 'Jo.' (Joseph?) Cooke's *Greene's Tu Quoque* (Queen Anne's, 1611). Spendall begins, like Chartley, with a rather engaging gusto in his prodigality, but the tone changes when he is arrested. The punk, bawd, and pander who flattered him and preyed on him now reject him with the characteristic brutality of the outlaw world, and he is taken to prison, where his misery is conveyed in small but telling details. He has no money, and must beg at the 'hole,' feeding 'out of the alms-basket, where charity appears in likeness of a piece of stinking fish' (p. 258). Finally he delivers a long, moralizing speech of repentance:

O, what a slave was I unto my pleasures!
How drown'd in sin, and overwhelm'd in lust!

That I could write my repentance to the world,
And force th'impression of it in the hearts
Of you of my acquaintance ...
Let all avoid false strumpets, dice, and drink;
For he that leaps i'th'mud, shall quickly sink. (pp. 260–1)

We are in the world of moral drama, but not for long.

Spendall is saved from prison by the widow Raysby, who charitably pays his debts. His first reaction seems to be a resolve to spend a life of honest industry, but this impression soon disappears. He decides to repair his fortunes by marrying the widow; in order to accomplish this, he breaks into her bedroom, threatens her with a dagger, and demands not only instant betrothal but instant consummation. She binds him to a bedpost, and rails at him; when he refuses to curse her in return, she suddenly unbinds him, declares that she was merely testing him, and accepts his proposal. He, in his turn, says that he never actually intended to *use* the dagger, and the incident concludes amicably. The prodigal is just as rash and wildbrained as ever, if not more so, but this time he gets away completely with his conduct. The morality has suddenly evaporated. Cooke seems to be experimenting with different attitudes to the prodigal story without fusing these attitudes into a coherent whole. The final impression, however, is that if the prodigal is lively enough and cheeky enough the dramatist can allow him to get away with anything.

But if Cooke could not make up his mind to sweep the moral presentation out of the way altogether, other playwrights could. The lively young rake who forestalls moral judgment by amusing the audience provides easy, natural material for comedy, and we find him over and over again, not just in prodigal plays, but in many of the intrigue comedies considered in the next chapter. There is a special piquancy in cases where the play includes conventions from the 'straight' prodigal story, turned upside-down by their new context. Heywood's *If You Know Not Me, You Know Nobody, Part Two* (Queen Anne's, 1605) is a case in point. Jack Gresham, the nephew of Thomas Gresham, has a penchant for dice and women, but even his uncle, the spokesman for middle-class virtue in the play, is won over by the young man's excuses for his conduct:

GRESHAM
He told me you bestow'd a gown of a strumpet.
JOHN
Why alas, uncle, the poor whore went naked, and you know the text commands us to clothe the naked; and deeds of mercy be imputed unto us for faults, God help the elect.

GRESHAM
Well, if your prodigal expenses be aim'd
At any virtuous and religious end,
'Tis the more tolerable; and I am proud
You can so probably excuse yourself. (p. 255)

With the paragon of citizens capitulating in this way, it is easy for the audience to follow suit; and Jack's speech, in which it is difficult to tell genuine good-heartedness from amusing impudence, makes it easier.

Even his theft of a hundred pounds from his uncle seems more a joke than a crime: Gresham's Puritan servant Timothy Thin-beard, who tries to stop the theft, is himself arrested by a trick, and driven to confess his own secret debaucheries, while Jack escapes scot-free to France, to spend the money in a brothel. A similar fate overtakes Old Hobson, Jack's employer, who tracks him to the brothel to lecture him on his misdeeds. The moral earnestness of the scene (already made precarious by the fact that Hobson has crossed the Channel in his dressing-gown and slippers) collapses completely when Jack has his employer arrested in a mock raid on the brothel, and treats him to the sort of lecture he really deserves himself: 'Nay, my mistress shall know't, that's flat. Are there not wenches enow in England, but you must walk over sea in your slippers, and venture (not being shod) to come into France a-wenching? What, an old man, too! She shall know what a slippery trick you would have served her in your slippers in France' (pp.314–15). The tables are turned on the would-be moral agent, who cheerfully admits defeat. Nor does Jack suffer the usual consequences of his debauchery: when his money is gone, he simply proposes to the rich widow Lady Ramsey, who, far from being offended by the impudent tone of his proposal, refuses him only because she has resolved not to marry again, and gives him enough money to pay his debts. Reform comes in its own good time, without the conventional preliminaries of suffering and repentance:

And now, i'faith, I have all my wild oats sown,
And if I can grow rich by help of this,
I'll say I rose by Lady Ramsey's kiss. (p. 332)

His prodigality is seen as part of the natural process of growing up, and he is evidently going to join the respectable world of prosperous citizens represented by his uncle – who was also a prodigal in his youth (p. 282). The story of Jack Gresham is an escapist fantasy in which the prodigal is immune from consequences, and those who try to correct him are rendered powerless; it functions as a holiday interlude in the pageant of civic responsibility presented by the rest of the play.

There is, in the end, a kind of rationale for Heywood's genial presentation of the prodigal: it is only natural for a young man to sow a few wild oats, and there is no need to get stuffy about it. But Heywood's presentation is relaxed and casual, one episode trailing loosely after another: the idea that there is a point to it all emerges only as an afterthought. Ben Jonson, who also uses prodigal conventions to make a point of his own, goes to work more purposefully. He seizes one particular plot device – that of the moral agent who tries to save the prodigal (a convention he uses straightforwardly in *The Staple of News*) – and gives it a searching, amusing critical examination in two of his earlier comedies. In *Every Man in his Humour* (Chamberlain's, 1598) Old Knowell disguises himself to observe and correct the follies (as he imagines them) of his son Edward and Edward's companion Wellbred. But in the end it is the father who is tricked and admits he was wrong:

Though I do taste this as a trick, put on me,
To punish my impertinent search, and justly;
And half forgive my son for the device. (IV.x.61–3)

As Justice Clement indicates, Edward is simply indulging in harmless fun, and his father's moral anxiety is out of all proportion to the offence: 'What? Your son is old enough to govern himself; let him run his course, it's the only way to make him a staid man. If he were an unthrift, a ruffian, a drunkard, or a licentious liver, then you had reason; you had reason to take care; but, being none of these, mirth's my witness, an I had twice so many cares as you have, I'd drown them all in a cup of sack' (III.vii. 86–92). Jonson is satirizing those who are over-fussy in the pursuit of morality, and he does so by taking one of the conventions of the prodigal play and turning it on its head.

This theme is further developed in the riotous, expansive comedy of *Bartholomew Fair* (Lady Elizabeth's, 1614). Here, a prodigal and a variety of would-be moral agents are among the characters drawn to the Fair, a world of knavery and sensuality where reason and morality collapse and the animal side of man rules unchecked. Without sentimentalizing the Fair, Jonson acknowledges its coarse vitality and the impossibility of imposing order on it. Bartholomew Cokes, the prodigal, sinks happily into the Fair, spending his money uncontrollably on trifles; as the play progresses he is systematically cheated and stripped in the conventional manner; but, unlike conventional prodigals, he remains unchastened and uneducated by the experience, and at the end of the play, when everyone troops home to Justice Overdo's house for supper, he insists on bringing the puppets along. It is not the prodigal but the moral agents who are corrected. Justice Overdo, spying in disguise on the 'enormities' of the Fair, treating the measuring of custards and other such trifles as matters of grave public consequence, is really feeding his sense of his own importance. Wasp, the servant whose job it is to keep Bartholomew under control, is equally self-important, and ill-tempered to boot. Overdo's role recalls the disguised, moralizing fathers of standard prodigal plays; Wasp suggests the honest servant who tries to keep his master out of trouble; but both are too foolishly self-important to carry any real moral weight, and are reduced to ineffectual grumbling. With the hypocritical Puritan Zeal-of-the-Land Busy, they end up in the stocks. The disgrace of this destroys Wasp's authority over Bartholomew and he sits down to watch the puppets with his charge. Adam Overdo is equally crushed to find his own wife parading in a strumpet's gown. He learns, in the words of the gamester Quarlous, 'you are but Adam, flesh and blood! You have your frailty, forget your other name of Overdo' (v.vi.96–8).

The scope of *Bartholomew Fair* is, of course, far wider than that of a simple prodigal play, or even an upside-down prodigal play. But Jonson's reversal of some of the conventions of the prodigal story provides an important indication of his purpose. The anti-prodigal morality, with its disapproval of dicing, drinking, and wenching, runs the risk of denying simple animal fun, and Jonson warns us against taking that risk. He is not positively defending prodigality or knavery (after all, there is no keener critic of these than Jonson himself, when he is in the vein); what he is trying to do, I think, is to achieve a balanced outlook, that will permit man to take the full measure of his own nature, including its animal side.

There are two of Fletcher's comedies which take not merely a few conventions but the whole moral pattern of the standard prodigal story and turn it systematically upside down, so that a new code emerges. Valentine, in *Wit Without Money* (Lady Elizabeth's? c. 1614) is a prodigal by philosophical conviction. He is fed up with the social responsibilities imposed by land and money, and, to the despair of his more practical relatives, spends his estate recklessly. His uncle laments, 'Alas, he's sunk, his means are gone, he wants, and which is worse, / Takes a delight in doing so' (i.i.p.146). Other prodigals spend their money thinking only of the pleasures they are getting, and are shattered when they find they have left themselves with nothing. Valentine spends his money with the express purpose of leaving himself with nothing: 'How bravely now I live, how jocund, how near the first inheritance, without fears, how free from title-troubles!' (i.i.p.151). He insists that he will be able to get by simply on his own wit and personality: 'why, all good men's means, my wit's my plough

... every man's clothes fit me, the next fair lodging is but my next remove' (I.i.p.151). Fletcher makes this eccentric rebel both attractive and dramatically effective: a racy, engaging personality communicates itself through the speeches, and makes us willing to accept Valentine's philosophy, even when he is brushing off the real suffering which his irresponsibility creates for his tenants:

TENANTS
We beseech you for our poor children's sake.
VALENTINE
Who bid you get 'em? Have you not threshing work enough, but children must be bang'd out o'th'sheaf too? .(I.i.p.149)

The conventional sentimental appeal is mocked, and anyone who has ever felt like pushing an old lady under a streetcar will understand and approve.

The conventional plot is also mocked, as Valentine wins through, unchanged and unrepentant. In an important scene, he gives away most of his outer garments and accessories; it is the symbolic stripping of the prodigal, as in *The Staple of News*. But Valentine refuses to be cowed. He justifies his nakedness to his uncle as a sign of his freedom, making another of his references to the state of primal innocence: 'Freemen, uncle, ought to appear like innocents, Old Adam, a fair fig leaf sufficient' (III.i.p.179). He admits, in soliloquy, that he is cold, and needs to find some new clothes fairly soon; yet even as he says this he is rescued, and we see that he was right when he predicted he could live simply by being himself. He finds a suit that has been left for him by the widow Lady Hartwell, who has taken a fancy to him. His uncle, who sees himself as a moral agent, expects that the stripping will have a corrective effect: 'his spirit must be bowed, and now we have him, have him at that we hoped for' (IV.i.p.181) – and a few lines later Valentine enters wearing his new clothes. The moral correction that works in other plays is exploded in a comic anticlimax.

Fletcher provides an even more detailed reversal of the conventions in *The Scornful Lady* (Queen's Revels? c. 1613). Young Loveless rejoices in the apparent death of his elder brother, since he has his own plans for the estate: 'We'll have it all in drink, let meat and lodging go, they are transitory, and show men merely mortal; then we'll have wenches, every one his wench, and every week a fresh one; we'll keep no powder'd flesh.' (I.ii.113–16). The mock-religious touch in the language strikes a note of engaging impudence; Young Loveless, like Valentine, has created his own morality. He has two moral agents trying to reclaim him; the more prominent of these is the high-minded steward Savil, who tries unsuccessfully to dissuade him from his rioting. Young Loveless does not merely ignore him; he tempts him to join in the debauchery – and, after some initial reluctance, Savil succumbs. When the Elder Loveless returns to see what has been happening to his estate, he denounces the steward, quite unfairly, as a corrupter of youth who has been feeding the prodigal's riots, and threatens him with dismissal. The convention of the honest servant is turned completely upside down: Savil finds himself wandering in despair, like a fallen prodigal, and begging Young Loveless for help. The latter delivers a brief lecture to him, and the comic inversion of the convention is complete: 'This is your drinking and your whoring, Savil, I told you of it, but your heart was hardened' (v.iii.22–3).

The other moral agent is the prodigal's elder brother, who, behaving as fathers do in other plays, goes away, disguises himself, returns to announce his own death, and, after the situation thus created has developed to the point at which somebody can be accused of something, removes the disguise and chastises the offender. This is the classic pattern; except that the Elder Loveless chastises the wrong offender. The prodigal's offences are dismissed in one line: 'you have been wild and ignorant, pray mend it' (iii.ii.192–3). It is Savil who bears the brunt of the attack, a tirade against drunkenness and lechery several speeches long, which ends: 'You may walk and gather cresses, sir, to cool your liver; there's something for you to begin a diet, you'll have the pox else. Speed you well, Sir Savil; you may eat at my house to preserve life; but keep no fornications in the stables' (iii.ii.217–21). Once again, the convention is turned upside down. The moral fervour is directed, with comic injustice, against the wrong man.

Finally, Young Loveless is married to a widow, who will be able to maintain him – another convention. She hopes that marriage will reform him and bring him back to respectable society, and in that hope urges him to get rid of his drinking companions. In most prodigal plays, this hope would have been fulfilled. But Young Loveless replies, 'I will be short and pithy: I had rather / Cast you off by the way of charge' (iv.ii.49–50). Far from being shocked by this, the widow acquiesces, and enters into the spirit of the rioters: 'And my good friends, since I do know your diet, / I'll take an order, meat shall not offend you, / You shall have ale' (iv.ii.102–4). As in *Wit Without Money*, prodigality wins through, unrepentant and uncorrected.

By far the subtlest and most elaborate parody of the standard prodigal story is to be found in *Eastward Ho* (Queen's Revels, 1605), by Chapman, Jonson, and Marston. A bare plot outline might indicate that we were dealing with a straightforward prodigal play, and in fact this is how some critics have taken it.[6] The merchant Touchstone has 'two prentices: the one of a boundless prodigality, the other of a most hopeful industry. So have I only two daughters: the eldest, of a proud ambition and nice wantonness; the other of a modest humility and comely soberness' (1.i.81–5). The characters and their fates are neatly balanced: the industrious apprentice Golding marries the worthy daughter Mildred, and, by a series of rapid promotions, becomes an alderman's deputy. The idle apprentice Quicksilver (the names reinforce the neatly patterned quality of the story) is involved in a number of harebrained schemes to raise money, including a voyage to Virginia planned by the bankrupt knight Sir Petronel Flash; the apprentice and the knight are shipwrecked on the Thames, and end up in prison. Girtred, Touchstone's foolish daughter, whose head has been turned by books of chivalry, marries Sir Petronel, deluded by dreams of a castle in the country, and ends up homeless and destitute. This sounds like material for a straightforward moral play; but an examination of the way the story is *presented* may lead to a different view.

Quicksilver's behaviour is that of a copybook prodigal – spendthrift, drunken, roistering, and scornful of all good advice. He brings to his swaggering a flair that makes, theatrically, a refreshing change from the wholesome maxims of Touchstone and Golding. His advice to Golding is typical: 'Why, do nothing, be like a gentleman, be idle, the curse of man is labour. Wipe thy bum with testones, and make ducks and drakes with shillings; what, Eastward ho! Wilt thou cry, what is't ye lack? Stand with a bare pate, and a dropping nose, under a wooden penthouse, and art a gentleman? Wilt thou bear tankards, and may'st bear arms?' (1.i.118–24). He may be a fool, but he cuts a dash. Girtred certainly *is* a fool, and has none of Quicksilver's wit, but her social ambitions (fostered by her equally foolish mother) are more amusing than offensive:

GIRTRED
Aye mother, I must be a lady tomorrow; and by your leave mother (I speak it not without my duty, but only in the right of my husband) I must take place of you, mother.
MRS. TOUCHSTONE
That you shall, Lady-daughter, and have a coach as well as I too.
GIRTRED
Yes mother. But by your leave mother (I speak it not without my duty, but only in my husband's right) my coach-horses must take the wall of your coach-horses. (1.ii.105–13)

6 See, for example, Thomas Marc Parrott, Introduction to his edition of *The Plays and Poems of George Chapman*, II (London, 1914), 840; Julia Hamlet Harris, Introduction to her edition of *Eastward Ho* (New Haven, 1926), p. xxiii; and Louis B. Wright, *Middle-Class Culture in Elizabethan England* (Chapel Hill, 1935), pp. 630–1.

This is no calculating social climber but a child indulging in pre-Christmas fantasies, and lording it over her less imaginative playmates. The folly of Quicksilver and Girtred is quite clear, but it is difficult to work up severe moral indignation against them, or to feel they deserve any punishment beyond the comic explosion of their dreams.

And the morality of thrift and industry by which they are judged and found wanting is not allowed the kind of authority it would have been given in a standard prodigal play. Usually this morality is simply assumed, or briefly stated, as a standard of judgment agreed on by the playwright and the audience. Here, however, it is fully dramatized, and we are led to examine it in a way that makes simple assent impossible. Touchstone misses no opportunity to promote the citizen virtues of thrift and industry, and to present himself as an example of what can be achieved:

And as for my rising by other men's fall, God shield me. Did I gain my wealth by ordinaries? No. By exchanging of gold? No. By keeping of gallants' company? No. I hired me a little shop, fought low, took small gain, kept no debt book, garnished my shop for want of plate with good wholesome thrifty sentences: as, *Touchstone, keep thy shop, and thy shop will keep thee. Light gains makes heavy purses. 'Tis good to be merry and wise* ... And I grew up, and I praise Providence, I bear my brows now as high as the best of my neighbours. (I.i.44–51, 55–7)

One might think that a character like this, who is 'merry and wise,' who upholds virtue without being solemn about it, could be taken as a guide to our sympathies throughout. One thinks of such citizen-hero figures as Simon Eyre and Old Hobson. But Touchstone's preaching becomes comic through sheer repetition, and Quicksilver's remark, 'Well said, old Touchstone, I am proud to hear thee enter a set speech i'faith, forth I beseech thee' (III.ii.128–9), indicates that the parody is deliberate.

But at least Touchstone is a comparatively genial figure, for all his moralizing; the presentation of Golding and Mildred is somewhat sharper. There is no fun in them: their natures are so shrunken that a cool-headed moralizing is all they are capable of. Their love for each other is stated with such unimpeachable propriety that we wonder if they actually *enjoy* the idea of getting married; and when Touchstone offers then a marriage feast as sumptuous as that which his wife gave Girtred, Golding replies,

Let me beseech you no, sir, the superfluity and cold meat left at their nuptials will with bounty furnish ours. The grossest prodigality is superfluous cost of the belly; nor would

I wish any invitement of states and friends, only your reverend presence and witness shall sufficiently grace and confirm us.

TOUCHSTONE

Son to my own bosom, take her and my blessing ... (ii.i.156–63)

The speed with which Touchstone accepts Golding's offer is a little suspicious, but at least he was prepared to spend some money on the wedding. Golding's plan is a cheap and insipid way to celebrate a marriage, and it shows how incomplete the morality of thrift is as a guide to living.

In fact, the most effective criticism of the prodigal group comes from inside. We hear a note of weary realism from Quicksilver's punk Syndefy, who rebukes the prodigal for his carelessness about money (ii.ii.55–6, 87–90) and Girtred for her 'pretty waking dreams' (v.i.91); and from Sir Petronel, who is constantly aware of the pinch of necessity and who is equally sardonic about his wife's fantasies (ii.ii.230–5) and Quicksilver's schemes for getting rich: 'I like his spirit rarely, but I see no means he has to support that spirit' (iv.i.205–6). This quiet, realistic criticism seems more in proportion to the offence than the relentless moralizing of Touchstone and Golding, just as simple disillusionment seems a more appropriate punishment for the prodigals than the conventional imprisonment and threat of death. But in the case of Quicksilver the full apparatus of the standard prodigal story is produced and set in motion – trial, imprisonment, and repentance in the shadow of the gallows. The playwrights are not content with Fletcher's comparatively simple trick of turning the story upside down; they preserve the story intact, and even expand upon it: the discomfiture of the prodigals is more detailed and elaborate than in the conventional plays. But the increased elaboration has the same effect as in the presentation of Touchstone and Golding: the attention to detail is sly and ironic, and we find it impossible to take the story seriously.

The crisis in the prodigals' affairs is signalled, appropriately, by the storm that breaks up the Virginia expedition before it even leaves England. Slitgut, watching from a safe vantage point at Cuckold's Haven, remarks, 'Lord! What a coil the Thames keeps! She bears some unjust burthen I believe, that she kicks and curvets thus to cast it' (iv.i.13–15). But this is not *King Lear* or *The Tempest*, and 'unjust burthen' is comically excessive. The prodigals are merely paying the price of the folly that has exposed them to this danger, and the prevailing tone of the scene is mocking, as the location at Cuckold's Haven suggests. Various characters are washed ashore at heavily symbolic locations: the usurer Security (who has brought his own wife to Sir Petronel for a last fling, thinking she was someone else's) lands at Cuckold's Haven; and Quicksilver is pulled ashore at the gallows at Wapping. The characters' reactions are also comically excessive: Security compares himself to the Serpent of Eden (iv.i.45–54), while Quicksilver delivers a passionate speech of repentance (iv.i.120–9), only to bounce back a few moments later with an elaborate scheme for getting rich by blanching copper. Although Girtred is not involved directly in the storm, the play is so managed that her disappointment over her castle in the country appears to coincide with it; and she also overreacts to her fate, retreating deeper into storybook fantasy as she becomes disillusioned with her knight: 'Would the Knight o' the Sun, or Palmerin of England, have us'd their ladies so, Syn? Or Sir Lancelot? Or Sir Tristram?' (v.i.29–31).

But success brings its fantasies, no less than failure does. As the prodigals sink into misery, Golding's rise begins, and Touchstone – like Girtred – begins to confuse real life with legend:

Worshipful son! I cannot contain myself, I must tell thee, I hope to see thee one o' the monuments of the city, and reckon'd among her worthies, to be remembered the same day with the Lady Ramsey, and grave Gresham, when the famous fable of Whittington and his puss shall be forgotten, and thou and thy acts become the posies for hospitals, when thy name shall be written upon conduits, and thy deeds play'd i' thy lifetime, by the best companies of actors, and be call'd their get-penny. This I divine. This I prophesy. (iv.ii.68–77)

Heywood's play about Gresham was first acted around the same time as *Eastward Ho*, and there may be a direct allusion to it here. In any case, Touchstone is starting to live in a world of fiction: he wants life to duplicate the plays he has seen. Just as he wants Golding to be a theatrical citizen-hero, he wants Quicksilver to suffer the fate of the fictional prodigal: 'Of sloth cometh pleasure, of pleasure cometh riot, of riot comes whoring, of whoring comes spending, of spending comes want, of want comes theft, of theft comes hanging; and there is my Quicksilver fixt' (iv.ii.324–8). The sequence has the simple inevitability of the prodigal ballads so popular at the time. In the final scene, Quicksilver's fellow prisoners expect him to be hanged, not because of anything he has done, but because Touchstone wants to see him hanged (v.v.1–8). The application of fictional conventions to life can, one feels, be carried too far.

In the final prison sequences we find a magnificent parody of the sort of prodigal stories Touchstone has evidently been reading. Quicksilver too is getting his behaviour from books; in his repentant phase 'He can tell you almost all the stories of the *Book of Martyrs*, and speak you all the *Sick Man's Salve* without book' (v.ii.56–8). He sings a wonderfully inept ballad of repentance, to the tune of *I wail in woe, I plunge in pain*. Furthermore, the literary conventions collide amusingly with reality. The gaoler Wolf, whose name recalls the hard-hearted minions of the law in conventional plays, is a soft-hearted fellow who resents having his name used as an indication of his cruelty. The hymn-singing of the penitents, though it might be satisfying as a convention of sentimental fiction, is a distinct nuisance to the neighbourhood: 'They will sit you up all night singing of psalms, and edifying the whole prison; only Security sings a note too high sometimes, because he lies i' the twopenny ward, far off, and cannot take his tune. The neighbours can not rest for him, but come every morning to ask, what godly prisoners we have' (v.ii.46–51). There is also some sly fun at the expense of audiences who wallow in the repentances of stage characters: Quicksilver's fellow prisoners regard him with an awestruck admiration that recalls the foolish excitement of Mistress Fond and Mistress Gazer, the gossips who saw Girtred off to her castle in the country. And Touchstone himself is softened: 'Listen. I am ravished with his repentance, and could stand here a whole prenticeship to hear him' (v.v.109–10). One feels that he pardons Quicksilver not so much for moral reasons as because he finds him satisfying artistically. His change of heart is engineered by Golding, who is also keeping to a literary role – that of modest, unassuming benefactor who aids the distressed but wants his name kept out of it (v.ii.79–86).

Finally, the resolution of the play is achieved not by breaking the artistic conventions which have dominated the characters' behaviour, but simply by the introduction of another convention, that of the happy ending in which the prodigal is forgiven. This convention too is parodied: Touchstone, in his new benevolence, is as relentlessly aphoristic as ever – 'The ragged colt may prove a good horse' (v.v.73) – and Security sees all too quickly how mercy may be won: 'Pray you sir, if you'll be won with a song, hear my lamentable tune, too' (v.v.142–3). In the last analysis, the parody of the prodigal story becomes simply the vehicle for a deeper satire on those who see life in terms of theatrical conventions. The dialogue is full of joking allusions to other plays (*The Spanish Tragedy, Tamburlaine, Richard III, Hamlet* – all the old favourites) and this may indicate how the authors' minds are working. The theatrical parody is all-pervasive in the final scene as the characters settle comfortably into the roles they have created for themselves, and the only reality we can recognize is the crowded theatre that reminds us it was all a play:

TOUCHSTONE
            ... Now London, look about,
And in this moral, see thy glass run out:
Behold the careful father, thrifty son,
The solemn deeds, which each of us have done;

The usurer punish'd, and from fall so steep
The prodigal child reclaim'd, and the lost sheep.

QUICKSILVER

Stay sir, I perceive the multitude are gather'd together, to view our coming out at the counter. See, if the streets and the fronts of the houses be not stuck with people, and the windows fill'd with ladies, as on the solemn day of the Pageant!

O may you find in this our pageant, here,
The same contentment, which you came to seek;
And as that show but draws you once a year,
Let this attract you hither, once a week. (v.v.205–10, *Epilogue* 1–9)[7]

The play's real epilogue is not a moral tag, but an appeal for a long run.

In the citizen-hero and citizen-villain plays we considered in chapter 2, comedy and responsible social morality could be powerful allies. But we have now seen that the action of a comedy, and the judgments it draws from its audience, may not be restricted to the pious belief that money should be honestly got and responsibly used. The comic form is broad enough to support a wide range of sympathies, and the happy ending can be a triumph for the social bond and the responsibilities that go with it, or (as in Fletcher) for the witty individual who is concerned only with his own pleasures. But even the happy ending itself, as part of a conventional structure, may be open to ridicule: life is never as neat as comedy makes it, and in *Eastward Ho* we see a comedy making precisely that admission, turning comic form itself into an object of satire.[8]

7 The effect of this moment is well described by M.C. Bradbrook in *The Growth and Structure of Elizabethan Comedy* (Harmondsworth, 1963): 'And then, with a sudden jerk, actors and audience are turned out of the theatre into the street, the artifice is broken: the galleries become windows and the yard a lane' (p. 150).

8 There is another case of theatrical burlesque of the prodigal figure in Beaumont's *The Knight of the Burning Pestle* (Queen's Revels? *c*. 1607). In the play within the play, Old Merrythought revels comfortably in his own home, while his thrifty wife and son (like prodigals in conventional plays) wander the streets, lost and helpless. In the end, they have to beg him to let them in, which he does only after they have sung a catch. This is part of the play's burlesque of various kinds of popular drama, but – like Fletcher, and unlike the authors of *Eastward Ho* – Beaumont makes his point by turning the story itself upside down. For a fuller discussion of Beaumont's play from this point of view, see John Doebler, 'Beaumont's *The Knight of the Burning Pestle* and the Prodigal Son Plays,' *SEL*,v (Spring 1965), 333–44.

4

The comedy of intrigue: money and land

BLACK KNIGHT'S PAWN
Sir, your plot's discovered.
BLACK KNIGHT
Which of the twenty thousand and nine hundred
Four score and five, canst tell?
Middleton, *A Game at Chess*

The last two chapters have examined the way in which certain theatrical type-figures – the citizen-hero, the usurer, the prodigal – are used to embody attitudes, respectable or otherwise, to the handling of money. But the fascination with money that runs through citizen comedy is shown most frequently in comedies of intrigue, where we watch characters in competition with each other, with money and property as the prizes. In this chapter the range of attitudes that can be embodied in comedies of intrigue will be examined, and particular consideration will be given to the way in which an amoral delight in trickery can disrupt conventional values.

For at the bottom of the comedy of intrigue is a sporting fascination with the game itself, as we see, for example, in *Wit at Several Weapons* (auspices unknown, c. 1609) – a play of doubtful authorship[1] which traditionally belongs to the Beaumont and Fletcher canon. A usurer cuts off his son's allowance, and threatens to disinherit him unless he demonstrates convincingly that he can live

---

1 Middleton and Rowley are often suggested as having had a share in the writing: see Cyrus Hoy, 'The Shares of Fletcher and his Collaborators in the Beaumont and Fletcher Canon (v),' *SB*, XIII (1960), 89.

by his wits. The son proves his mettle by repeatedly cheating his father, who shows a sporting appreciation for the young man's skill, and at the end of the play distributes money among his accomplices, remarking,

> wealth, love me as I love wit;
> When I die,
> I'll build an Alms-house for decay'd wits. (v.i.p.141)

There is also the simple but solid pleasure of watching a natural victim get what is coming to him. In the subplot of John Marston's *The Dutch Courtesan* (Queen's Revels, *c.* 1604) the 'witty city jester' Cocledemoy plays a series of tricks on the sharking vintner Mulligrub, simply because Mulligrub lends himself to that sort of thing: he is a Puritan and a snob; he cheats his customers; and best of all, he flies into a glorious temper when enraged. At the end, Cocledemoy returns what he has stolen, explaining, 'All has been done for emphasis of wit' (v.iii.136).[2]

Plays like these show the comedy of intrigue in its most basic form, provoking a simple delight in the skill of the trickster and the discomfiture of the victim. No serious feelings are engaged, as we see in the speed with which all is forgiven at the end. In both cases, we are told quite explicitly that what matters is the display of wit. But there are other comedies in which the intrigue provokes a more complex response, combining the sporting pleasure of the game itself with a commentary on the society in which the game is played. Three plays in particular – Middleton's *A Trick to Catch the Old One*, Barry's *Ram Alley*, and Massinger's *A New Way to Pay Old Debts* – are worth considering from this point of view. They involve figures we have already examined – the prodigal and the usurer – and they share essentially the same plot. Yet they are very far from provoking the same pattern of responses in the audience. In each case, a different kind of social and moral analysis is built around the basic intrigue plot.

In *A Trick to Catch the Old One* (Paul's, *c.* 1605), a young prodigal, Witgood, recovers by trickery the land he had lost to a usurer, his uncle Lucre. Witgood pretends that he is about to marry a rich widow (really the Courtesan, his ex-mistress) and Lucre, thinking to cheat the widow as well, does everything he can to further the match, including restoring Witgood's lands. Meanwhile Lucre's rival and fellow-usurer, Hoard, is tricked into marrying the so-called

---

2 In the Cambridge comedy *Club Law* (Clare Hall, Cambridge, *c.* 1599), the citizens of 'Athens' (a very thin disguise for the English university town) are likewise subjected to a series of practical jokes, simply for being what they are. This, however, is a special case, for the play is a contribution to the local town-and-gown war.

widow. The audience's feelings should be solidly engaged: our sympathy for the prodigal as an engaging wastrel, as a victim, and finally as a clever rogue combines with our antipathy to the usurer, who has removed land from its rightful owner.

Witgood begins the play as a fallen prodigal, faced with the loss of his land (I.i.1–7). But instead of repenting in the usual way and begging to be restored to respectable society, he continues to use the outlaw world of debauchery as a base from which to attack the well-to-do. His accomplices are clearly associated with his old prodigal days: the Host, on joining the conspiracy, says, 'and if I stand you not in stead, why then let an host come off *hic et haec hostis*, a deadly enemy to dice, drink, and venery' (I.ii.50–2). The Courtesan speaks of their project in appropriate language: 'Though you beget, 'tis I must help to breed' (I.i.57). And he accepts her offer of loyal support with a cheerful, flippant 'Spoke like an honest drab, i'faith' (I.i.52). There is a feeling of the more disreputable elements of society banding together to attack the establishment, and there is something attractive in their mutual loyalty and *esprit de corps*.

The rogue is witty and attractive, the plot is ingenious, and all this wins our support, as we might expect. Somewhat less predictable, however, is Middleton's treatment of the usurers. Lucre and Hoard are just what their names indicate. Witgood gives us a pungent description of his uncle, whose scorn of prodigality is combined with a greed that leads him to exploit the prodigal:

But where's Long-acre? In my uncle's conscience, which is three years' voyage about; he that sets out upon his conscience ne'er finds the way home again, he is either swallowed in the quicksands of law-quillets, or splits upon the piles of a *praemunire*; yet these old fox-brained and ox-browed uncles have still defences for their avarice, and apologies for their practices, and will thus greet our follies:

> He that doth his youth expose
> To brothel, drink, and danger,
> Let him that is his nearest kin,
> Cheat him before a stranger.

And that's his uncle, 'tis a principle in usury. (I.i.6–18)

Witgood's tone is jocular, and less bitter than we might expect; there is even a wry appreciation of his uncle's knavery. And this tone is maintained throughout the treatment of the usurers. The two have quarrelled, like dogs over a bone, about a young heir whom Hoard had been about to defraud when Lucre 'as his conscience mov'd him, knowing the poor gentleman, stept in between 'em, and cozened him himself' (I.i.118–20). They maintain their quarrel in a crotchety, cantankerous manner that is amusing to watch, and that gives them a certain liveliness. The important point is that they are so busy fighting one another they pose no serious threat to Witgood, and there is, accordingly, no animosity in his attitude towards them:

He has no conscience, faith, would laugh at them, they laugh at one another!
  Who then can be so cruel? troth, not I;
  I rather pity now, than ought envy;
I do conceive such joy in mine own happiness, I have no leisure yet, to laugh at their follies. (IV.ii.87–92)

This lack of malice contributes to Witgood's own attractiveness; it also gives a clue to the spirit in which the usurers are attacked. They have to be defeated in order for Witgood to achieve his ends, but this is simply part of the game, and is surprisingly uncoloured by personal spite; certainly they are more indulgent portraits than the savage caricatures of more conventional plays.

Hoard, in particular, is not one of those miserly usurers whose capacity for enjoyment has been deadened by greed; we can hardly see him as crabbed and life-denying. Expecting a wealthy marriage with the widow, he hires a tailor, a barber, a perfumer, and a huntsman to attend on him (IV.iv.21–74). His daydreams have a gleeful self-indulgence, and a loving attention to detail; he prides himself on having

not only a wife large in possessions, but spacious in content: she's rich, she's young, she's fair, she's wise; when I wake, I think of her lands – that revives me; when I go to bed, I dream of her beauty – and that's enough for me: she's worth four hundred a year in her very smock, if a man knew how to use it. But the journey will be all in troth into the country, to ride to her lands in state and order following; my brother, and other worshipful gentlemen, whose companies I ha' sent down for already, to ride along with us in their goodly decorum beards, their broad velvet cassocks, and chains of gold twice or thrice double; against which time I'll entertain some ten men of mine own into liveries, all of occupations or qualities; I will not keep an idle man about me: the sight of which will so vex my adversary Lucre – for we'll pass by his door of purpose, make a little stand for nonce, and have our horses curvet before the window – certainly he will never endure it, but run up and hang himself presently! (IV.iv.4–20)

Of course, the fact that Hoard's bride is really a penniless courtesan makes the whole speech ironic, especially the line, 'she's worth four hundred a year in her very smock, if a man knew how to use it,' which is true in a sense that Hoard does not suspect. But while we laugh at Hoard, the laughter is kept indulgent by the comic gusto he displays.

Certainly the presentation of Hoard and Lucre is quite lenient compared with the presentation of the dishonest lawyer Dampit. As R.B. Parker puts it, 'Dampit's mercenariness is basically no different from Hoard's or Lucre's, but the virulence of the attack on him is remarkable ... it appears to have been used as a safety-valve for disgust.'[3] Whatever moral outrage Middleton may have felt at the world he depicts is here drained off into a subplot which is never properly integrated with the rest of the play, but which at least succeeds in preserving the light tone of the main action. There is also a fairly sharp portrayal of the cruelty of materialism in Witgood's creditors, who take a sadistic pleasure in the idea of arrest: 'Oh, 'tis a secret delight we have amongst us; we that are used to keep birds in cages, have the heart to keep men in prison, I warrant you' (IV.iii.49–51). But this is a small touch in passing, and again it does not affect the presentation of Hoard and Lucre.

Greed is attacked in the main plot, but Middleton's weapon is comic irony, and our response is laughter. Greed may not dull the usurers' capacity for enjoyment, but it does dull their cunning; they are so eager to seize the bait that they do not see the trap. Lucre, in his eagerness to make Witgood a fatter morsel for his avarice, restores his lands and, we feel certain, will not get them back. Hoard marries the widow in haste, to forestall Witgood, and finds he has married a whore. But we should notice the kind of judgment that is being passed: greed as we see it here is not so much a vice as a folly. The standard of judgment is efficiency, not morality. There are also social prejudices invoked: a hint of town-versus-country, of citizen-versus-gentry. But again this issue, while unquestionably there, is not raised so explicitly as we shall see it raised in the more earnest comedies of *Michaelmas Term* and *A New Way to Pay Old Debts*. The contest is one of wits more than of class against class or virtue against vice.

Finally, the fact that there are two victims instead of one (as in the plays to be discussed shortly) has the effect of dissipating the pressure on them: neither is the object of really concentrated scorn, and they share the comic punishments between them, Lucre losing the lands and Hoard marrying the Courtesan. This means, among other things, that they themselves take their defeats in a cheerful and sporting manner. Towards the end of the play Lucre and Witgood slip into an easy, friendly relationship; the older man seems more delighted at Hoard's discomfiture than chagrined at his own. Hoard himself, though he has married a punk, ends the play with a note of festivity and a cheerful acceptance of his own fate: 'So, so, all friends, the wedding-dinner cools: / Who seem most crafty

---

3 'Middleton's Experiments with Comedy and Judgement,' *Stratford-upon-Avon Studies I: Jacobean Theatre*, ed. John Russell Brown and Bernard Harris (London, 1960), p. 188.

prove oft times most fools' (v.ii.196–7). The usurers react, not like men who have suffered grave personal misfortunes, but like men who have lost a game.

For a play that shows a fiercely competitive world of knavery, *A Trick to Catch the Old One* is surprisingly good-tempered. The brisk, catchy title sets the tone, and the dialogue is full of cheerful aphorisms which reduce the affairs of men in society to a series of predictable patterns of gulling and being gulled: 'I perceive there's nothing conjures up wit sooner than poverty, and nothing lays it down sooner than wealth and lechery' (iii.i.86–8). The generalizing quality of speeches like this establishes an aura of coolness and detachment: as a result, the game of knavery is played with a minimum of real animosity, and without rousing in the audience any deep sense of moral outrage against the world it depicts.

David, Lord Barry's *Ram Alley* (King's Revels, *c.* 1608), owes much of its plot to *A Trick to Catch the Old One*. But it uses the plot as a vehicle for a more detailed and pungent satire than Middleton attempts in the earlier play, and there are sharper reactions expected from the audience than a sporting appreciation of the game. Barry makes some changes in the story, the most important being that the two usurer-victims are combined into one. William Small-shanks, a young prodigal who has lost his money and lands, mostly through lechery, pretends that he is about to be married to a rich lady, the heiress Constantia Somerfield, who is in fact impersonated by his punk Frances. Throat, the usuring lawyer who has Small-shanks' lands, is tempted by the idea of marrying the heiress himself. The young man then pretends to be arrested for debt, and accepts, with an amusing show of reluctance, Throat's offer to bail him and restore his mortgage in return for taking over Small-shanks' rights to the heiress. Throat suffers both the punishments that were divided between Hoard and Lucre: loss of the lands, and marriage to a whore.

There is, then, more pressure directed against Throat; and the presentation of the character himself is far less indulgent. This is a more concrete satiric portrayal than that of Hoard or Lucre. The latter two were greedy old men with usuring tendencies; that was all we needed to know in order to enjoy their discomfiture, and beyond this Middleton did not attempt to particularize their vices or comment on them in detail. But we learn quite a bit about Throat's career and profession. He is, by his own admission, the 'dregs and off scum of the law' (i.i.p.288). He has become rich through a variety of squalid means, including usury, and Small-shanks, who is a gentleman, denounces him as a social upstart:

Why, wert thou not begot (thou foolish knave)
By a poor sumner on a serjeant's widow?

Wert thou not a Puritan, and put in trust
To gather relief for the distress'd Geneva[ns]?
And didst thou not leave thy poor brethren,
And run away with all the money? Speak,
Was not that thy first rising? (v.i.p.378)

The gentlemanly scorn implied in this speech is the attitude from which Barry presents this character throughout. His eagerness to marry Constantia Somerfield is partly greed and partly social ambition:

My fate looks big! methinks I see already
Nineteen gold chains, seventeen great beards, and ten
Reverend bald heads, proclaim my way before me.
My coach shall now go prancing through Cheapside,
And not be forc'd to hurry through the streets
For fear of serjeants. (iii.i.p.334)

There are obvious similarities with Hoard's daydream – including, of course, the irony of the situation, which undermines both speeches. But Throat's vision is narrower, more intensely focused on the trappings of social vanity, and its basic impulse seems to be not so much enjoyment as self-assertion. While Hoard talks of sharing his pleasure with his fellow-citizens, Throat imagines himself in solitary splendour, surrounded by lackeys. Therefore his gusto, unlike that of Middleton's usurer, does not communicate itself to us, and we remain in an attitude of satiric detachment.

Throat looks particularly foolish when his dreams collide with reality. Thinking he has married the heiress, he calls on her mother, the aristocratic Lady Somerfield. One of the servants describes his behaviour:

I think him lunatic; for he demands
What plate of his is stirring i' the house!
He calls your men his butlers, cooks, and stewards:
Kisses your women, and makes exceeding much
Of your coachman's wife. (iv.i.p.355)

Lady Somerfield is not amused:

Hence, you base knave! you petty-fogging groom!
Clad in old ends, and piec'd with brokery:
You wed my my daughter! (iv.i.p.356)

Hoard, for all the irony surrounding his marriage, was never made to look quite such a fool as this; Barry sees to it that his usurer is not merely defeated, but humiliated. Throat, like Middleton's usurers, is mocked for his inefficiency in the intrigue. But he is mocked for his manners as well. There is still little, if any, moral basis to the satire: Throat is not so much wrong as squalid and gauche. He has dreams above his station, and he misbehaves in a great lady's house. This is one of the clearest examples we have – clearer, I think, than any in Middleton – of satire with a distinct class bias.

There is also a clearer sense than in *A Trick to Catch the Old One* that the knavery of the play's action is a mirror of the knavery in the world at large. Middleton's play includes comments on the way of the world, but they tend to be crisp and economical, tossed off in passing. Barry, on the other hand, frequently stops the action to let one of the characters deliver a substantial set piece on the knavery or lechery of the world. Throat's definition of the law, for example, is clearly a general comment, not just a description of his own shady practice:

I tell thee, fool, it is the kingdom's nose,
By which she smells out all these rich transgressors:
Nor is't of flesh, but merely made of wax,
And 'tis within the power of us lawyers
To wrest this nose of wax which way we please:
Or it may be, as thou say'st, an eye indeed;
But if it be, 'tis (sure) a woman's eye,
That's ever rolling. (i.i.p.288)

Barry is not particularly disturbed by the corruption of the world; he seems to find it amusing, and sometimes – especially when lechery is the theme – the comedy conveys a sense of gleeful participation. Even a speech to establish the time becomes a joke about sex: 'By Jove, the night grows dark, and Luna looks / As if this hour some fifty cuckolds were making' (iv.i.p.353).

Accordingly William Small-shanks, who is both knave and lecher, is seen not just as winning a game but as meeting a corrupt world on its own terms. Announcing his plan to cheat his father of a wealthy widow by marrying her himself, he delivers what I take to be the key speech of the play:

What, though I cheat my father; all men have sins,
Though in their several kinds: all ends in this –
So they get gold, they care not whose it is.
Begging the court, use bears the city out,

Lawyers their quirks: thus goes the world about.
So that our villainies have but different shapes,
Th'effect's all one, and poor men are but apes
To imitate their betters: this is the difference –
All great men's sins must still be humoured,
And poor men's vices largely punished.
The privilege that great men have in evil,
Is this, they go unpunish'd to the devil.
Therefore I'll in; this chain I know will move;
Gold and rich stones win coyest ladies' love. (v.i.pp.359–60)

For a few moments Small-shanks stands apart from the whirligig of knavery, commenting on it with a spectator's detachment. For a couple of lines, he almost sounds serious about the dilemma of the less privileged in a world where money is power. But the detachment is shortlived, for Small-shanks' essential response to the knavery of the world is to join in – and off he goes to cheat his father of the widow.

Small-shanks' knavery, like the debauchery of Fletcher's prodigal heroes, is depicted as a philosophy in its own right, which the character can stand by proudly. When his punk Frances, masquerading as the heiress, is introduced to William's father, the following dialogue ensues:

WILLIAM SMALL-SHANKS
Beg his chain, wench. (*Aside*)
BEARD
Will you cheat your father?
WILLIAM SMALL-SHANKS
Aye, by this light, will I. (ii.i.p.296)

Small-shanks reacts in a similar way when the widow challenges him about his sexual morality:

TAFFATA
I dare not wed; men say y'are naught, you'll cheat,
And you do keep a whore.
WILLIAM SMALL-SHANKS
That is a lie;
She keeps herself and me. (v.i.p.364)

One cannot help warming to a character who describes himself so frankly, and who is so completely free of humbug. He sticks by his vices with the sort of

dignity one usually associates with those who advocate a simple, honest way
of life:

> I tell you, sir,
> Your best retired life is an honest punk
> In a thatch'd house with garlic: tell not me:
> My punk's my punk, and noble lechery
> Sticks by a man when all his friends forsake him. (i.i.p.273)

Immorality has become codified, with its own inverted sense of integrity. This
is expressed more seriously in the sense of honour and mutual loyalty that binds
Small-shanks and his associates together. He and his punk express a definite
feeling of obligation to each other; and even his friend Boutcher, who disap-
proves of Small-shanks' lechery, offers unqualified support when he hears his
friend is going to attempt the recovery of his land: 'take; there's my store. /
To friends all things are common; (i.i.p.276). Small-shanks reciprocates by
sharing his takings with Boutcher as soon as his plans start to bear fruit
(ii.i.p.298). In a world of predatory knaves they have banded together to prey
as a group, and this, together with their superior efficiency, gives them the edge
over Throat, in comic appeal as well as effectiveness.[4]

Small-shanks also stands very much on the dignity of his social position. His
loyalty to his punk is partly a matter of a gentleman keeping his word
(i.i.pp.274–5). The generosity of Boutcher is contrasted with the meanness of
citizens who refuse to help a fallen prodigal. Small-shanks suspects his friend,
who has lectured him on his dissolute ways, of developing middle-class attitudes
generally, and is relieved to find that this is not the case:

> You are like our citizens to men in need,
> Which cry, 'tis pity a proper gentleman
> Should want money; yet not an usuring slave
> Will lend him a denier to help his wants.
> Will you lend me forty shillings?
> BOUTCHER
> I will.
> WILLIAM SMALL-SHANKS
> Why, God-a-mercy, there's some goodness in thee. (i.i.p.275)

There is a feeling that in the world of knavery, gentlemen at least should stick
together; and we have seen already the note of class animosity in Small-shanks'

---

4 See John V. Curry, *Deception in Elizabethan Comedy* (Chicago, 1955), p. 58.

attitude to Throat. The play as a whole has a distinct anti-citizen bias; at one point Adriana, the widow's maid, makes a passing, gratuitous reference to 'a snivelling citizen' (i.i.p.278). Throat, as usurer, belongs to this group, and this is a factor in weighting sympathy against him. For Barry, citizens are, quite simply, fair game.

At the end of *A Trick to Catch the Old One*, the prodigal hero gets his girl, and there is some suggestion that his marriage will restore him to social respectability in the conventional manner (v.ii.180–95), but this suggestion is underplayed. Not content with underplaying the idea, Barry goes one step farther and makes Small-shanks' marriage not a stabilizing factor, but one more expression of the character's buccaneering knavery. He steals the widow from his father, through motives which are not romantic, but sensual and mercenary:

Well, I like this widow: a lusty plump drab:
Has substance both in breech and purse,
And pity and sin it were she should be wed
To a furr'd cloak and a night-cap. I'll have her:
This widow I will have: her money
Shall pay my debts, and set me up again. (iv.i.p.342)

He gives her long and racy lectures on the obvious disadvantages of marrying his father:

if you do wed the stinkard,
You shall find the tale of Tantalus
To be no fable, widow. (iv.i.p.341)

Finally, he bursts into her bedroom and demands, 'Resolve, wed me, and take me to your bed, / Or by my soul I'll straight cut off your head' (v.i.p.363). When she agrees to marry him, he insists on bedding her at once: 'A bird in hand – you know the proverb, widow' (v.i.p.364). The scene is practically identical with Spendall's rough courtship of the widow in *Greene's Tu Quoque*, but here it is perfectly in tune with the rest of the play.

Felix E. Schelling calls *Ram Alley* 'among the very best imitations of Middleton's comedy, and a better play than several of Middleton's own.'[5] Certainly there are ways in which it goes beyond its model, *A Trick to Catch the Old One*. Its plotting is much less neat and economical, but it creates a more pungent

5 *Elizabethan Drama 1558–1642* (New York, 1959), i, 519

satiric picture of society. The response it evokes, however, is entirely amoral: our sympathy is enlisted for a hero who, instead of battling the vices of society, uses those vices for his own ends. There are few plays of the period in which moral considerations are so successfully excluded; a codified, gentlemanly immorality becomes the norm of judgment. The world of *Ram Alley* is a limited one, and some may find it offensive, but it is both vivid and coherent, true to its own internal laws.

Massinger, in *A New Way to Pay Old Debts* (Red Bull Company? 1621), also uses Middleton's basic plot line, and also employs it as a vehicle for commentary. But just as Overreach is a more serious and disturbing villain than Hoard, Lucre, or Throat, so the tone throughout is quite different from that of the other two plays, especially the raffish gusto of *Ram Alley*, and the nature of the commentary is also quite different. An important basis of the play's judgment is the opposition of two sets of values: money on the one hand (represented by Overreach) and birth and breeding on the other. This opposition, and the superiority of birth, are stated most clearly by Lady Allworth, trying to dissuade Lord Lovell from marrying Overreach's daughter:

As you are noble (howe'er common men
Make sordid wealth the object, and sole end
Of their industrious aims) 'twill not agree
With those of eminent blood (who are engag'd
More to prefer their honours, than to increase
The state left to 'em, by their ancestors)
To study large additions to their fortunes
And quite neglect their births: though I must grant
Riches well got to be a useful servant,
But a bad master. (IV.i.180–9)

The sober, sententious tone of this speech indicates the problem that Massinger has set himself. He is trying to combine an intrigue plot which Middleton and Barry used in amoral comedies of knavery with the earnest assertion of some rather dignified social principles.

We see this problem first of all in the depiction of Wellborn, the prodigal gentleman who lost his lands to Overreach before the play began, and whose plot to get them back constitutes the main action. Lady Allworth warns her stepson Tom against keeping company with him,

Not cause he's poor, that rather claims your pity,
But that he's in his manners so debauch'd
And hath to wicked courses sold himself. (I.ii.120–2)

But Wellborn makes a different kind of appeal from that made by Small-shanks and Witgood. He does not cheerfully acknowledge his own debauchery, or claim our support by the wit and ingenuity of his knavery. He appeals, instead, to our sympathy for him as a victim, and to a sense of nobility in those who may be willing to help him. The innkeeper Tapwell, whom Wellborn himself set up in business, is typical of the hypocritical rogues who have exploited him and then rejected him:

For from the tavern to the taphouse, all
On forfeiture of their licenses stand bound,
Never to remember who their best guests were,
If they grew poor like you. (1.i.811–14)

Tapwell upbraids Wellborn with his own debauchery, but Wellborn, though he cannot deny the charge, brushes it aside: 'Some curate hath penn'd this invective, mongrel, / And you have studied it' (1.i.52–3). His reply is to berate Tapwell for his ingratitude, and to beat him off the stage. Instead of revelling in his prodigality, Wellborn prefers to see himself as a man who has been exploited, and who has a grievance to avenge. This is valid as far as it goes, but the lack of self-criticism is a little disturbing. He criticizes Tapwell for employing whores, but he fails to criticize himself for frequenting them.

Two scenes later, when he appeals to Lady Allworth for help in recovering his estate, a similar evasiveness can be detected. At first she refuses to listen to him. He treats her contempt as a reflection on his poverty, not his debauchery (though she herself had said that he was not to be despised for poverty); he appeals to her not to scorn him simply because he is in rags, and reminds her of his noble birth:

You will grant
The blood that runs in this arm, is as noble
As that which fills your veins; those costly jewels,
And those rich clothes you wear; your men's observance,
And women's flattery, are in you no virtues,
Nor these rags, with my poverty, in me vices. (1.iii.87–92)

He then goes on to remind her of his friendship for her late husband, who had also been down on his luck:

'Twas I that gave him fashion; mine the sword
That did on all occasions second his;

I brought him on and off with honour, lady:
And when in all men's judgements he was sunk,
And in his own hopes not to be buoy'd up,
I stepp'd unto him, took him by the hand,
And set him upright. (I.iii.103–9)

The appeal to gratitude for old friendship is logical enough, and one feels that
Lady Allworth is right to yield to it, as she does. The dignified movement of
the speech, and the appeals to honour, suggest that this friendship is something
quite different from the raffish camaraderie of Small-shanks and Witgood. On
its own terms, however, it might be just as acceptable, were it not for the fact
that it sits rather strangely with what we have heard of Wellborn's dissolute
ways. Once again Wellborn, in appealing for sympathy, has ignored the real
objections to him. Lady Allworth, in this scene, also ignores her own earlier
criticisms of his debauchery, and allows him to defend himself as though the
only charge he had to answer were poverty. The intrigue plot, inherited from
Middleton, postulates a prodigal hero who has lost his lands through dissipation
but who is, somehow, attractive. Massinger, concerned with the values of birth
and breeding, tries to make Wellborn sympathetic on the grounds of gentlemanly dignity, thus denying himself the Middleton-Barry solution of making
the prodigality itself attractive in an amoral way. The prodigality, in fact,
becomes an embarrassment, and in trying to ignore it Wellborn puts himself
in a false position; it is, accordingly, a little difficult to offer him the whole-
hearted sympathy one feels for Witgood.
  Wellborn's plan is essentially similar to those of Witgood and Small-shanks.
He creates the impression that he is going to be married to Lady Allworth, and
on the strength of this Overreach lends him a thousand pounds, thinking that
he can claim Lady Allworth's land as security. His greed overreaches itself, for
he parts with the money and gets nothing in return. There is some satire on
the power of money in society when Wellborn assumes the role of Lady
Allworth's lover; the prospect of money not only makes Overreach and his creature Marrall suddenly obsequious, but gives society as a whole a new respect
for Wellborn. Tapwell, afraid of what he might do to him, comments,

When he was rogue Wellborn, no man would believe him,
And then his information could not hurt us.
But now he is right worshipful again,
Who dares but doubt his testimony? (IV.ii.13–16)

It is significant that Wellborn himself does not consider his name properly cleared until he has righted himself in a gentlemanly way, by going to war at the end of the play; the prestige conferred by payment of his debts is treated ironically, as showing the mercenary nature of the world.[6] Breeding, not money, is the real value.

So far, this is satisfying and dramatically logical. Wellborn's imposture reveals the materialism of society, and tempts and chastises the greed of Overreach. But the manner in which Overreach's defeat is brought about is much less satisfactory. Marrall, attracted by Wellborn's new prosperity, and tired of his rough treatment by Overreach, offers his services to Wellborn. He predicts that Overreach will ask him for security on his loan of a thousand pounds, and advises him not to offer any, but to claim instead that Overreach owes him ten times as much – the value, in fact, of the land the usurer got from Wellborn in the latter's prodigal days. Wellborn follows these instructions carefully, and when Overreach produces the deed by which Wellborn signed the land over to him, he finds it is nothing but a blank parchment. This, of course, is Marrall's doing. Overreach is cheated, not only of the thousand pounds, but of Wellborn's land as well. But there is something trivial in the manner of the cheating – 'certain minerals / Incorporated in the ink, and wax' (v.i.330–1). Overreach is such a powerful villain that one would like to see him defeated by something more significant than a chemical reaction. He has not, in the end, been tripped up by his own greed, but by the machinations of Marrall.

Wellborn's use of Marrall points to an acute problem in the play. He, and the other gentry, continually denounce Overreach and all his works. Yet he unashamedly uses Overreach's creature, and is quite willing to have his land recovered by means that the usurer himself might employ. This would be perfectly acceptable if Wellborn himself were presented as a rogue who could disarm criticism by the wit and flair he brought to his knavery. But such is not the case: with his high-mindedness and nobility, he cuts rather a sober figure, and his use of Marrall brings him dangerously close to hypocrisy. Particularly disturbing, I think, is the way he leads Marrall on, promising him land and office, and once he has served his turn, dismisses him abruptly with a moral lecture:

You are a rascal, he that dares be false
To a master, though unjust, will ne'er be true
To any other: look not for reward,
Or favour from me, I will shun thy sight
As I would do a basilisk's. (v.i.338–42)

6 Esther Cloudman Dunn, in *Ben Jonson's Art: Elizabethan Life and Literature as Reflected Therein* (Northampton, Mass., 1925), p. 136, feels this is the underlying theme of the play. It is, I think, an aspect of the larger theme of money versus breeding.

This deception seems to underline the falseness of Wellborn's moral position.

Lovell and Lady Allworth also practise dissimulation in their attempts to defeat the usurer. In neither case is the deception as questionable as Wellborn's use of Marrall, and one might accept their actions, as one accepts Wellborn's earlier actions, save for one thing. The characters raise doubts themselves. The Lady, asking Lovell why he is pretending courtship to Margaret when he has no intention of marrying her, comments,

> Dissimulation but ties false knots
> On that straight line, by which you hitherto
> Have measur'd all your actions. (IV.i.229–31)

He asks her in turn why she has dropped her mourning and is pretending to pay court to Wellborn; both justify their actions on the grounds that their ends are good. One would simply have accepted this as a matter of course – if only the point had not been raised specifically. This may seem paradoxical, but in a play that appeals so continually to one's moral sense, it is unfortunate that two of the more virtuous characters have been made to state openly that the end justifies the means. One feels, as one does with Wellborn, that the intrigue against Overreach defeats him only in a mechanical way, and fails to provide the clear moral opposition that his villainy demands. In a pure comedy of knavery, this would not matter; but it does matter in play whose tone is so morally earnest.

Massinger's use of Middleton's plot is partly to blame, for it inevitably involves the characters in chicanery. Also at fault, I think, is his reliance on birth and breeding as values to set in opposition to Overreach. Not only does this sit uneasily with the intrigue plot (as in Wellborn's appeals for sympathy); it also fails to provide even the sort of verbal opposition we should like. For example, when Overreach offers to get Lady Allworth's land for Lovell, the latter replies,

> I dare not own
> What's by unjust, and cruel means extorted.
> My fame, and credit are more dear to me,
> Than so to expose 'em to be censur'd by
> The public voice. (IV.i.83–7)

The concern for one's reputation as a gentleman seems an inadequate response to Overreach's monstrous offer. Class awareness as a standard of judgment works well enough in the play's peripheral comic scenes, as when Lady Allworth's servants (in a scene recalling the humiliation of Throat) laugh at

Marrall's table manners (II.ii.118–32); but, as a standard on which to base the central confrontation of good and evil, it breaks down. What works in *Ram Alley* will not do for the more serious atmosphere of *A New Way to Pay Old Debts*.[7]

The plot skeleton which Massinger found in Middleton and Barry demanded a certain amount of knavery from the usurer's enemies; Massinger's own temperament gave the same characters a tendency to sober moralizing and appeals to honour; and the two do not fuse successfully. The villain is a powerful and frightening creation, but the moral opposition to him is somewhat weakened by the demands of intrigue comedy. In *A Trick to Catch the Old One* and *Ram Alley*, moral responses were kept firmly in check and we were allowed, in the first play, to enjoy the game, and in the second, to take an amoral delight in comtemplating the knavery of the world. Massinger's play, through containing a contradiction that is neither resolved nor exploited creatively, seems less satisfying by comparison, and indicates the dangers of imposing the wrong kind of seriousness on an intrigue comedy – or more precisely, perhaps, of embedding an intrigue comedy in a serious moral drama.[8]

The problem is not so much whether an intrigue comedy can bear a weight of commentary – *Ram Alley* shows that it can – but what *kind* of commentary it can bear. A satiric vision of the knavery of the world is easy enough to accommodate, but the desire to assert serious moral standards does not sit well with the essentially amoral premises of the intrigue plot. The same problem can be seen in another way in plays in which the tables are finally turned against the central intriguer. In the three plays just considered, the hero works throughout the action towards a definite goal, and the audience is encouraged to expect, and to welcome, his final success; a kind of team spirit is invoked. But there is another kind of structure in which the play is dominated by a trickster who, after a series of victories over the dupes, is finally outwitted himself. Here, the audience's sympathies must be more delicately adjusted, if the play is to give pleasure. We must enjoy the trickster's successes, and yet find satisfaction in his ultimate defeat. And the problem is further complicated, as we shall see, if this adjustment includes an attempt to assert moral considerations.

---

7 There is a valuable analysis of Massinger's failure to provide adequate opposition for Overreach in D.J. Enright, 'Poetic Satire and Satire in Verse,' *Scrutiny*, XVIII (Winter 1951–2), 222–3. Enright points out the superiority of *Volpone* in this respect.

8 Middleton himself failed in a similar way in his later comedy *No Wit, No Help, Like a Woman's* (Lady Elizabeth's? *c.* 1613). Here, the Low-waters have been cheated by the usurer Sir Avarice Goldenfleece, who is dead when the play opens. Mistress Low-water alternates between sentimental laments over her fallen state and witty knavery in cheating the usurer's widow. There is no attempt to modulate from one to another, and the effect is as though passages from two quite different plays had been arbitrarily put together.

Two plays by Middleton show quite different approaches to this problem. The main plot of *A Mad World, My Masters* (Paul's, *c.* 1606) has the genial temper of *A Trick to Catch the Old One* and seems, at first, to be presenting a similar action. Follywit's campaign against his uncle Sir Bounteous Progress is the characteristic young man's revenge on a close-fisted elder: Sir Bounteous has promised Follywit his estate when he dies, but refuses to give him anything for the present (I.i.41–55). There is even a hint that the old man has been a usurer in his time, and that Follywit is administering rough justice on him, but the reiterated 'if' in Follywit's speech keeps this indefinite: 'I am sure my grand-sire ne'er got his money worse in his life than I got it from him. If ever he did cozen the simple, why I was born to revenge their quarrel; if ever oppress the widow, I, a fatherless child, have done as much for him. And so 'tis through the world either in jest or earnest. Let the usurer look for't; for craft recoils in the end, like an overcharg'd musket, and maims the very hand that puts fire to't' (III.iii.5–12). Middleton has a purpose in keeping this charge of usury doubtful. Certainly the impression of Sir Bounteous from his actual appearances in the play (as distinct from what Follywit says about him) is of a lively, genial old man whose obsession, far from being the hoarding of money, is an extravagant sense of hospitality. Though he is open to criticism in that he seems interested in being hospitable only to lords (III.iii.20–3) his reckless generosity makes him engaging, a prodigal who can afford his prodigality. And he has a streak of raffishness in him, in keeping the courtesan Frank Gullman, that also recalls the conventional prodigal.

One expects, from past experience of such plays, that the young prodigal will emerge triumphant; but in our reaction to both sides, sympathies are about equal. Consequently the ending, in which the tables are turned on Follywit (the first half of his name begins to assert itself at the expense of the second), has the value of surprise, without really disappointing us. We accept it as simply one more amusing twist to the plot. The actual presentation of Follywit's defeat makes this acceptance easier, for Middleton is at his most inventive here. The game element of *A Trick to Catch the Old One*, with its ironic interplay of fact and deception, and its lack of emotional involvement, is strongly present. Folly-wit and his companions, having, in disguise, gulled Sir Bounteous of his watch and other valuables, return in their own shapes. Sir Bounteous is just describing the outrage when the alarm of the watch rings in Follywit's pocket, all is revealed, and the laughter is against the rogues. Follywit exclaims in chagrin, 'Have I 'scaped the constable to be brought in by the watch?' (v.ii.230). He then attempts to excuse himself by saying that he has taken a wife (which he has), whom he describes as 'a gentlewoman and a virgin' (v.ii.248) (which he genuinely thinks she is), and that this is to be taken as an earnest of the sober, reformed life he intends to lead. This wife turns out, to the delight of Sir

Bounteous, to be the courtesan Frank Gullman. Follywit has been deluded by the courtesan and her mother into the sort of marriage normally reserved as a punishment for usurers. His own prediction about the craft of the usurer recoiling upon itself is ironically recalled in the last couplet of the play, spoken by Sir Bounteous: 'Who lives by cunning, mark it, his fate's cast; / When he has gull'd all, then is himself the last' (v.ii.271–2). The game is over, there are no hard feelings, and Sir Bounteous gives his grandson a thousand marks as a dowry with his new wife, so that the young man has, after all, achieved his original purpose, though not by means he would have chosen himself. Follywit's defeat is the defeat of one particular rogue, but not of roguery in general. Those who triumph over him – Sir Bounteous and Frank Gullman – are just as engaging as he is, and their victory is, accordingly, satisfying by the comic standards of the play.

But in *Michaelmas Term* (Paul's, *c.* 1606) Middleton, like Massinger, gets into trouble through trying to accommodate the intrigue plot to serious moral commentary. Quomodo, the central intriguer, is a linen-draper who practises usury on the side. His chief purpose is to gain land from decayed members of the gentry, in order to raise his prestige among his fellow citizens:[9]

Now shall I be divulg'd a landed man
Throughout the livery; one points, another whispers,
A third frets inwardly, let him fret and hang! (iii.iv.5–7)

Like Hoard, he daydreams with infectious zest of enjoying his new social position (iv.i.70–7). His main intrigue is conducted against Easy, a gullible young gentleman from the country, and his conduct of this intrigue adds to his amoral comic appeal. One cannot help admiring a deception worked out in such loving detail, and operating with such deadly efficiency; and our satisfaction is increased by the stupidity of the victim, who plays so completely into Quomodo's hands that there seems to be a rough poetic justice in his final defeat.

Middleton, however, is not content to leave it at that. Quomodo, as a greedy and social-climbing usurer, is the sort of character who is normally attacked and put on the defensive in Jacobean comedy, as we have seen. His activities, amus-

9 The nature of the prestige conferred by owning land is suggested by Lawrence Stone, *The Crisis of the Aristocracy 1558–1641* (Oxford, 1965): 'the division between the gentleman and the rest was basic to Elizabethan society. An essential prerequisite for membership of the *élite* was financial independence, the capacity to live idly without the necessity of undertaking manual, mechanic, or even professional tasks' (p. 50). Quomodo, besides having a country place for pleasure, will enjoy a gentlemanly income from his rents.

ing though they are to watch, are socially disruptive: a gentleman's property is his by descent, and should as a matter of duty be passed to his heirs. As the foolish gallant Rearage cries, having lost at dice: 'Forgive me, my posterity yet ungotten!' (ii.i.121). And at times the language (for which Middleton is often given too little credit)[10] provides a quiet, insistent moral commentary. Quomodo speaks of his plot as

> the fairest to cleave the heir in twain,
> I mean his title; to murder his estate,
> Stifle his right in some detested prison. (i.i.102–4)

The implication is that land taken from its rightful owner is, in a sense, destroyed; and the wording of the speech shows that the gulling of Easy, though amusing, has also a latent brutality. A more overt judgment on Quomodo comes when he attempts to ensure the permanence of what he has gained. In order to find out how his son Sim will treat the land when he inherits it, and in order to test the loyalty of his household (his way of life obviously is not conducive to mutual trust) he feigns death, 'because I see before mine eyes that most of our heirs prove notorious rioters after our deaths, and that cozenage in the father wheels about to folly in the son ... being awake in these knowings, why should not I oppose 'em now, and break destiny of her custom, preventing that by policy, which without it must needs be destiny?' (iv.i.81–91). 'Destiny' operates just as he feared it might: Sim turns out to be as gullible as Easy, and Quomodo's henchman Shortyard (whom he regarded as a valued and trusted servant) has, in no time at all, cheated him of the land. Even Shortyard's success is shortlived, for Easy has him arrested almost immediately, and repossesses his land. The principle that what is dishonestly got cannot be kept asserts itself with the inevitability of natural law.

If Middleton had stopped there, he might have achieved a fairly satisfying balance of judgment and comic indulgence. But in the last act he hits Quomodo too hard. Suddenly and inexplicably, the linen-draper becomes a maladroit fool, and the former gull Easy becomes suprisingly efficient; in the final court scene, Quomodo loses everything, and his henchmen Shortyard and Falselight are sentenced to banishment. In A Mad World, My Masters the defeat of the central intriguer carried no moral weight; it was just one more move in a game of knavery played by the entire cast, and it did not demand any radical change in the audience's sympathies. Here, however, the turning of the tables not only

10 See, for example, L.C. Knights, Drama and Society in the Age of Jonson (Harmondsworth, 1962), p. 217.

forces the characters into new and unconvincing roles, but assumes more hostility to Quomodo on the part of the audience that the play has actually aroused, and takes too little account of the fun he has provided.[11] At the last moment, Middleton's anxiety to make a moral point throws the intrigue comedy off balance.[12]

It is against the last-minute breakdown of an otherwise intelligent and amusing play like *Michaelmas Term* that we can appreciate the achievement of Ben Jonson's *The Alchemist* (King's, 1610). Here, the audience's sympathies are finely adjusted, and the last-minute reversal is entirely satisfying. But this is a larger achievement than *A Mad World, My Masters*, for Jonson has also attained the success which eluded Middleton and Massinger in using the intrigue plot as a vehicle for moral commentary.

In fact, cheating and moral analysis are so thoroughly fused that any criticism which tries to discuss them separately is bound to give a misleading impression of the play. In Lovewit's house greed is both exploited and exposed. The confidence games run by Face, Subtle, and Doll Common are based on W.C. Fields's dictum that you can't cheat an honest man: behind the variety of motives the dupes profess is the lowest common denominator of greed. And each deception is carefully attuned to its victim, exposing his character while it empties his pockets – as when Doll reveals Mammon's uncontrollable lechery, or the brethren are led to announce that 'Casting of dollars is concluded lawful' (iv.vii.44). An interesting symptom of this is the number of times Subtle imitates his victims to their faces, trading fake pieties with Mammon, melting in awe before Dapper's supernatural powers, and competing with Ananias in a fanatical edginess about trifles. Lovewit's house is a hall of mirrors. And, ironically, the cheaters are caught before the mirrors themselves, since the greed they exploit in their victims is the force that drives them too.

All the same, we find ourselves taking sides. The confidence tricks are jokes shared with the audience. When Subtle says to Drugger,

11 See Parker, 'Middleton's Experiments,' p. 183.
12 Another play that loses its balance by turning the action too sharply against the central intriguer is the anonymous *The Puritan* (Paul's, 1606). The young scholar Pye-board intrigues against the family of a lately deceased usurer; he and one of his compatriots are about to seal their success by marrying the widow and her daughter when a noble reveals their deception and arranges safe, respectable matches for the women instead. Throughout the play everything has been done to rouse our sympathies in favour of the young scoundrels and against the usurer's family, and their final defeat is simply disappointing. This play is sometimes attributed to Middleton, but the evidence that has so far been presented, though interesting, is far from conclusive. See Wibur D. Dunkel, 'The Authorship of *The Puritan*,' PMLA, xlv (September 1930), 804–8; and Marilyn L. Williamson, 'Middleton's Workmanship and the Authorship of *The Puritan*,' NQ (February 1957), pp. 50–1.

Make me your door, then, south, your broad side, west,
And, on the east side of your shop, aloft,
Write *Mathlai, Tarmiel,* and *Baraborat;*
Upon the north part, *Rael, Velel, Thiel,*
They are the names of those Mercurial spirits
That do fright flies from boxes. (1.iii.63–8)

Subtle knows it is nonsense; we know it is nonsense; but Drugger does not. The same can be said of the changes – the alchemy, if you like – that transform the rogues into something more than they are. Subtle becomes a powerful wizard, Face a captain, and Doll the Queen of Faery. We, like the rogues, know these transformations for the cheats they are; our amusement springs from sharing with them a knowledge that the gulls lack; and this makes us, in a way, parties to the conspiracy.

There is also, in the case of Sir Epicure Mammon in particular, a moral judgment that makes us see him as particularly ripe for punishment. His orgiastic daydreams of what he will do with the philosopher's stone reveal viciousness on a grand scale; the greed and dishonesty of the cheaters are largely amusing, but when these qualities are blown up as grotesquely as they are in Mammon the effect is distinctly unsettling. His selfishness is not merely an inward-turning force; it turns outward as well, and its intentions are socially destructive:

Where I spy
A wealthy citizen, or rich lawyer
Have a sublim'd pure wife, unto that fellow
I'll send a thousand pound, to be my cuckold.

FACE

And I shall carry it?

MAMMON

No. I'll ha' no bawds,
But fathers, and mothers. They will do it best,
Best of all others. And my flatterers
Shall be the pure, and gravest of divines
That I can get for money. (11.ii.53–61)

His hypocritical piety also invokes a very serious range of values against which to judge him:

I shall employ it in all pious uses,
Founding of colleges, and grammar schools,

Marrying young virgins, building hospitals,
And, now and then, a church. (II.iii.49–52)

This is the citizen-hero code of social conduct, stated with comic exaggeration (and, in the last line, comic bathos) but stated nonetheless.[13] This code, as Mammon's language suggests, is religious as well as social, and throughout the play he is a figure not just of greed but of impiety and idolatry,[14] in whom folly and evil are indistinguishable.

The discomfiture of the dupes is satisfying by the standards of morality, and by the amoral standards of intrigue comedy. But the cozeners are judged as well. While the greed of the gulls leads them into sacrificing their possessions in the hope of gain, the greed of the cheaters leads to the break-up of their confederacy. In the end, Face cheats the other two and the only consolation they have is that they escape with their skins whole. Jonson prepares us for this in the quarrel in the opening scene, the memory of which creates a tension, a sense of danger, beneath the smoothly running operations of the rogues. With the appearance of Dame Pliant, the rift widens again, with Subtle and Face each wanting her for himself, and Doll kept uninformed. Finally, when Lovewit returns, the bubble bursts, and the splendid commonwealth of cheaters simply disappears.[15] Lovewit's return is an outside event triggering the explosion, but we have seen that the commonwealth contained within itself the seeds of its own destruction. This is similar to Quomodo's overreaching and Shortyard's treachery at the end of *Michaelmas Term*; greed is judged as self-destructive.

But the ending of *The Alchemist* is quite different from that of Middleton's play, for Jonson, in settling the fates of his characters, takes account of the delight the roguery has given, and the result is carefully balanced. Subtle and Doll lose their takings, but they escape other punishment. Face is reduced to his former position as a butler, but he keeps the money. Even the comparatively honest figures are carefully disposed of. Dame Pliant is won, not by the killjoy Surly, but by Lovewit, who is willing to turn a lenient eye on roguery. Surly is clear-sighted in his assessment of the rogues, but in criticizing them he throws cold water on the schemes that have been amusing the audience, and he himself is deficient in wit and initiative. When he tries to expose the con-

13 This point is developed at length by Alan C. Dessen, '*The Alchemist*: Jonson's "Estates" Play,' *Renaissance Drama*, VII (1964), 39–43.
14 See Myrddin Jones, 'Sir Epicure Mammon: A Study in "Spiritual Fornication,"' *Renaissance Quarterly*, XXII (Autumn 1969), 233–42.
15 This part of the play is well described by Edward B. Partridge, *The Broken Compass* (London, 1958), p. 117.

spiracy, the dupes drive him off the stage (IV.vii.1–62), and when he tries to win Dame Pliant he is weak on follow-through. Lovewit lectures him:

Good faith, now, she does blame you extremely, and says
You swore, and told her, you had ta'en the pains,
To dye your beard, and umbre o'er your face,
Borrowed a suit, and ruff, all for her love;
And then did nothing. What an oversight,
And want of putting forward, sir, was this!
Well fare an old Harquebusier, yet,
Could prime his powder, give fire, and hit,
All in a twinkling. (v.v.50–8)

Lovewit, while he has no illusions about what has been happening in his house, appreciates roguery and is no bad hand at it himself. And Kastril gladly accepts him as a father-in-law because he can quarrel, drink, and take tobacco with the best of them (v.v.131–45).

To describe the ending of *The Alchemist* as a compromise might suggest that something had been left out in order to achieve the right balance; but what one admires here, and throughout the play, is Jonson's masterly inclusiveness. The confidence tricks are amusing games *and* penetrating comments on the characters. The ending is a precise judgment which includes, as the ending of *Michaelmas Term* does not, a full acknowledgment of the value of wit. The comedy of intrigue can be a medium for social and moral comment, despite the comparative failures of Massinger and Middleton, and the comment can go deeper than Barry's wry acknowledgment that the world is full of cozenage. But to use the medium in this way, to see the game as a serious business at bottom, without for one minute losing sight of the *fun* of the game, demands a master craftsman who has taken the full measure of his art and can make a complex juggling trick look like a fluid, natural movement.

5
Who wears the breeches?

'More belongs to marriage than four bare legs under a blanket.'
Seventeenth-century proverb

Another standard form of intrigue plot is one in which a pair of young lovers
win each other after outwitting their parents, who have been trying to make
mercenary matches for them. The conventional sympathies of comedy are
activated: youth against age, love against money.[1] The plot-material has a long
theatrical history, particularly in the convention of the rival wooers. The
father's candidate for his daughter's hand is generally a fool – as in *Wily
Beguiled* (Paul's? *c.* 1602) and Cooke's *Greene's Tu Quoque* (Queen Anne's,
1611) – or an impotent old man – as in Fletcher's *The Night Walker* (Lady
Elizabeth's? *c.* 1611) and William Rowley's *A Match at Midnight* (Red Bull,
c. 1622). The lovers' opposition frequently includes a stereotyped usurer, who

---

1 To some extent, but not entirely, these are also the conventional sympathies of the tracts on
marriage that appear to have flooded the market in this period. Enforced and mercenary matches
are denounced by Thomas Heywood in *A Curtaine Lecture ...* (London, 1638): 'Others will
enforce them to marry where themselves like, and not where their children love; the effects
of which are commonly discontent and misery ... How often have forced contracts been made
to add land to land, not love to love? and to unite houses to houses, not hearts to hearts? which
hath been the occasion that men have turned monsters, and women devils' (pp. 99–100). This
is a characteristic statement. Equally characteristic, however, is Robert Cleaver's warning in
A godlie forme of hovsehold government ... (London, 1598): children, he writes, 'should not
... so much as give any liking, much less speech of marriage, without the consent of parents'
(p. 352). The only concession made to this in comedy is that parents usually bless the love-match
after it is too late to prevent it.

may be the father – as in William Haughton's *Englishmen for my Money* (Admiral's, 1598) – or the rival suitor, as in *The Night Walker*. The latter play is full of savage jokes about the usurer Algripe's physical grotesqueness and impotence:

Would you be content if you were young again,
To have a continual cough grow to your pillow?
A rottenness, that vaults are perfumes to,
Hang in your roof, and like a fog infect you?
Anointed hams, to keep his hinges turning,
Reek ever in your nose, and twenty night caps,
With twenty several sweats? (III.i.p.339)
ALGRIPE
... I must tell you a tale in our ear anon.
NURSE
Of Tom Thumb.
I believe that will prove your stiffest story. (I.i.p.322)

The stereotype which Algripe represents has a clear symbolic value – a figure of old age and sterility standing in the way of young love.

On the more tricky question of interclass marriage, the same values prevail. Such matches are clearly unsuitable if arranged by social-climbing parents – as in Davenport's *A New Trick to Cheat the Devil* (Queen Henrietta's? c. 1625) and Massinger's *A New Way to Pay Old Debts* (Red Bull Company? 1621) – and clearly acceptable if arranged by the lovers themselves.[2] In Dekker's *The Shoemakers' Holiday* (Admiral's, 1599) the parents of Lacy and Rose insist that class is a barrier, and even Simon Eyre urges Rose not to marry one of 'those silken fellows' (III.iii.41). But the lovers climb the class barrier, partly because Lacy meets Eyre's objection by becoming an honorary shoemaker in the course of the action,[3] but mostly because, as the King proclaims in the final scene,

Dost thou not know that love respects no blood?
Cares not for difference of birth, or state;
The maid is young, well-born, fair, virtuous,
A worthy bride for any gentleman. (V.V.103–6)

2 Marriage pamphlets are, of course, more cautious on the subject, insisting that the harmony and stability proper to marriage cannot be achieved in an interclass match: 'For as two horses, or two oxen, of unequal stature, cannot be coupled under one self-same yoke, so a noble woman, matching with a man of base estate, or contrarily, a gentleman with a beggar, cønnot be consorted and well matched under the bands of wedlock' (Cleaver, *godlie forme*, p. 148).
3 See L.C. Knights, *Drama and Society in the Age of Jonson* (Harmondsworth, 1962), p. 200.

It would, however, be misleading to suggest that there is any serious social thinking in these love-match comedies. The opposition to enforced, mercenary, and social-climbing matches is largely a matter of setting up the appropriate ground rules to enable the audience to enjoy the intrigue. Commentary is restricted to a few conventional remarks on the order of

> O God, how blind
> Are parents in our loves! So they have wealth
> They care not to what things they marry us. (*Greene's Tu Quoque*, p. 236)

and 'Title, my Lord, is a cold bed-fellow' (*A New Trick to Cheat the Devil*, II.i.p.215).[4] We are not expected to ask questions about the premises on which the intrigue is based. The actual marriage of the lovers is the fixed ending of a fixed dramatic structure, and we assume – if we think about it at all – that they live happily ever after. In other words, the Noah's Ark ending is a convention the audience must agree to accept; one of the easiest ways to burlesque a comedy is to imagine its young lovers after five years of marriage. The Elizabethans, of course, were aware of this: as Bacon wryly remarked, 'The stage is more beholding to Love, than the life of man,'[5] and in contemporary tracts on marriage there is a distinct mistrust of romantic love as a reason for getting married:

Some undergo this curse instead of blessing, merely for lust choosing their wives most unfitly, as adultresses, and such are said to marry by the eye, looking no further than a carnal beauty ... And for such a one so she be fair, and can kiss, she hath portion enough for such a pirate; but when this flower withers ... what shall continue love as then to the end, their winter sure shall be full of want, full of discontent, that thus grasshopper-like respected their summer.[6]

At this period, the Protestant, middle-class insistence that marriage was a dignified and important institution, and ought to be undertaken carefully with an eye to the personal happiness of the couple, was asserting itself against the

---

4 A possible exception is Middleton's early comedy *The Family of Love* (Admiral's? *c.* 1602) where the lovers Gerardine and Maria are allowed to go on at considerable length about the value of romantic love and the evils of enforced marriage, using a special high-flown style different from anything else in the play (see, for example, I.i.18–22 and III.i.26–33). But the ideas are still commonplaces, stated extensively rather than explored, and the fancy style, contrasted with the racy idiom of the rest of the play, raises the possibility of burlesque.
5 'Of Love,' *Essays*, ed. F.G. Selby (London, 1958), p. 23
6 Alexander Niccholes, *A Discourse, of Marriage and Wiving* ... (London, 1615), p. 7

older view, still practised by the aristocracy, of marriage as a property transaction.[7] Tracts on marriage appeared in great numbers, offering practical advice on choosing a mate and on living with her once you had her.[8] And the issue was taken up in the drama: domestic drama told sombre tales of marital disaster, like Wilkins' *The Miseries of Enforced Marriage* and Heywood's *A Woman Killed with Kindness*. Citizen comedy took up the theme in a lighter way: on the question of matchmaking, as we have seen, it had little to offer but a conventional plot formula. But on the question of what happens once the couple settles down to live together, we find a lively and varied range of treatments. In a sense, these plays look behind the conventional comic ending to examine what the final joining of hands actually signifies. And what they find, of course, is fresh material for a different kind of comedy.

In these plays, the conventional Elizabethan view of the proper balance of authority between husband and wife is not, as a rule, seriously questioned. Briefly, that view is as follows: order is as necessary in marriage as in a state, and the husband is the natural authority: 'Can this be counted slavery, or servile subjection? Must there not be in some subjection? Can all in a nation be kings?'[9] But that authority must be exercised humanely, without bullying: 'Wives are not to be made slaves but companions.'[10] This appears to have been an advance on the position of women in the rest of Europe: England was proverbially 'the paradise of women'[11] and visiting foreigners remarked that 'The women have much more liberty than perhaps in any other place; they also know well how to make use of it.'[12] Clearly, it demands a delicate adjustment to achieve the right balance, and the failure of that adjustment is promising material for drama.

One of the simplest forms this can take is that of the moralizing cautionary tale, similar to the straightforward prodigal plays discussed in chapter 3. Indeed, we often find the two motifs in the same play: the prodigal is also a bad husband who bullies his wife, and the wife is a Patient Griselda whose loyalty to her mate never wavers. We are given a black-and-white contrast, a simple moral diagram, characteristic of the moral comedies of the public theatres. A typical play

7 See Lawrence Stone, *The Crisis of the Aristocracy 1558–1641* (Oxford, 1965), p. 671.
8 See Louis B. Wright, *Middle-Class Culture in Elizabethan England* (Chapel Hill, 1935), pp. 201–27.
9 Ste. B., *Covnsel to the Hvsband: To the wife Instruction* ... (London, 1608), pp. 49–50. The title in itself indicates the relationship between husband and wife.
10 Richard Brathwait, *Ar't asleepe Husband? A Boulster Lecture* ... (London, 1640), p. 116
11 Morris Palmer Tilley, *A Dictionary of the Proverbs in England in the Sixteenth and Seventeenth Centuries* (Ann Arbor, 1950), s.v.E147
12 *England as Seen by Foreigners in the days of Elizabeth and James I*, ed. W.B. Rye (London, 1865), pp. 7–8

of this type is the anonymous *How a Man May Choose a Good Wife from a Bad* (Worcester's, *c.* 1602), sometimes attributed to Thomas Heywood. In this play, Arthur bullies and ill-treats his wife in a merciless fashion:

If thou wilt pleasure me, let me see thee less;
Grieve much; they say grief often shortens life:
Come not too near me, till I call thee, wife;
And that will be but seldom. I will tell thee,
How thou shalt win my heart – die suddenly,
And I'll become a lusty widower ... (i.ii.p.14)

If his brutality is arbitrary and mechanical, so also is the patience and meekness of his wife:

Sweet husband, if I be not fair enough
To please your eye, range where you list abroad,
Only, at coming home, speak me but fair:
...
If you delight to see me drudge and toil,
I'll be your drudge, because 'tis your delight. (i.ii.p.13)

In the treatment of the bullying husband there is no indulgence, and certainly no laughter: his offence is a very serious matter, all the more so in that he is abusing a wife who, being a model of patience, will not fight back.[13]

In Nathan Field's *Amends for Ladies* (Queen's Revels? *c.* 1611), Sir John Loveall, as part of an attempt to test his wife's fidelity, maltreats her to the point of beating her and giving all her clothes to a whore (iii.i.26–30). But though the husband's brutality is the usual one-dimensional villainy, there is a subtler statement of the wife's position than we sometimes get:

        for let him do
The most preposterous ill relishing things
To me, they seem good, since my husband does 'em,
Nor am I to revenge or govern him,
And thus it should be with all virtuous wives. (v.i.101–5)

And when he comes to her for forgiveness, she says, 'Rise, rise, sir, pray; /

---

13 There are similar treatments of the brutal husband in *The Fair Maid of Bristow* (King's, *c.* 1604) and S.S.'s *The Honest Lawyer* (Queen Anne's, *c.* 1615), both of which, like *How a Man May Choose*, are prodigal plays, in which the wife remains loyal despite her husband's behaviour.

You have done no wrong to me; at least, I think so' (v.i.134–5). She always makes it clear that she is speaking in her position as a wife, passing a special kind of judgment. His conduct *seems* good to *her*; *she* must not think he has wronged her. The implication is that anyone else is free to think or say what they like, but she in this case is not a private person with a judgment of her own; she is his wife and must submit. Field is not usually a subtle writer; but here he has gone beyond most other writers of moralizing comedy, and given us a glimpse of a real woman's face behind the mask of virtue. And this awareness of the wife's situation, denied the right to defend herself, makes the husband's behaviour seem all the more despicable.

We might expect more laughter in plays where the bullying is on the other side, for the shrewish wife is a well-established figure of fun. This is what we get, for example, in *Grim the Collier of Croydon* (Admiral's? 1600), possibly by William Haughton, in which a devil, sent from Hell to investigate the behaviour of women, marries a wife who proves to be too much for him. But to a suprising degree the shrew in comedy is presented as an object of serious concern, and treated in the same moralizing spirit as the bullying husband. In William Rowley's *A New Wonder, a Woman Never Vexed* (auspices unknown, *c.* 1625), Mistress Foster's continual nagging is directed towards making her husband more severe to his son Robin, who is, as she sees it, wasting the family revenues by aiding his prodigal uncle: 'I'd make / The one a stranger, the other a servant' (i.i.p.105). This attempt to break up the family is presented as a serious business; Robin speaks of 'the violent instigation / Of my cruel stepmother' (iii.i.p.151) and the severity of the language shows that here at least the shrew is no laughing matter. Nor does she really care about her husband; her reaction when he loses his money is quite ugly:

Let me curse somewhere, wretch, or else I'll throw
Them all on thee; 'tis thou, ungodly slave,
That art the mark unto the wrath of heaven:
I thriv'd ere I knew thee. (iii.i.p.160)

This play, by the way, emphasizes the dangers of treating marriage as a business affair; the match was a commercial one to begin with (i.i.p.104), and when the husband goes bankrupt, the wife, instead of comforting him, rejects him as a bad investment.

Rowley's is not the only treatment of the shrew as a serious threat. Mistress Changeable in Davenport's *A New Trick to Cheat the Devil* (Queen Henrietta's? *c.* 1625) usurps her husband's authority by insisting on her own unsuitable match for their daughter, and it takes Changeable most of the play, and a good deal of elaborate intrigue, to repair the damage. In the Lady Cressingham plot in Middleton's *Anything for a Quiet Life* (King's, c. 1621), in which Webster may have collaborated, the lady in question runs riot through her family, reducing her husband to a cipher, and forcing him to sell his land and to send his two children by a previous marriage out to board. The presentation of the shrew is earnest, even melodramatic, though in this case the effect is thrown away for the sake of an extremely unconvincing surprise ending (typical of the striving for superficial effects in these later Jacobean plays), in which it is revealed that Lady Cressingham's brutality to her family was only a pretence. But in the early scenes there are some shrewd comments on the social destructiveness of a bullying female. And behind all these earnest dramatizations of the shrew lies a very Elizabethan feeling that once order has been violated at any one point, widespread chaos follows.

These plays, like the standard prodigal plays whose nature they share, are comic largely by virtue of the happy ending, in this case the restoration of the proper balance of authority within the marriage. They examine the situation of the disrupted marriage through a series of simplified stock characters, designed to prove the appropriate moral points. A more subtle and interesting treatment is given in Henry Porter's *The Two Angry Women of Abington* (Admiral's, c. 1588), one of the best shrew comedies of the period. Here the characters are not moral paradigms but intractable human beings, each conceived as an individual. The play opens with a lively scene in which Mistress Barnes and Mistress Goursey fall out over a game of dice, each suspecting the other with her husband. Barnes, who is the host, tries to keep his wife under control:

Well, wife, you know it is no honest part
To entertain such guests with jests and wrongs:
What will the neighbouring country vulgar say,
When as they hear that you fell out at dinner?
Forsooth, they'll call it a pot-quarrel straight;
The best they'll name it is a woman's jangling.
Go to, be ruled, be ruled. (1.i.pp.103–4)

There is an appeal to the serious issues of reputation and hospitality (which in this case includes friendship between neighbours, a value asserted seriously throughout the play); at the same time there is a reminder of how ludicrous a brawling woman is. A balance is struck between earnest criticism and ridicule. Neither works, however, for Mistress Barnes replies sharply,

God's Lord, be ruled, be ruled!
What, think ye I have such a baby's wit,

To have a rod's correction for my tongue?
School infancy! I am of age to speak,
And I know when to speak. (I.i.p.104)

With its short, sharp exclamations, this speech is convincingly natural: we can hear the sound of the woman's voice. Mistress Goursey's technique is different, but equally striking, and rather more subtle. She retains the smooth facade of the obedient wife, but the lurking menace is unmistakeable :

Come, kind-hearted man,
That speaks his wife so fair – ay, now and then;
I know you would not for an hundred pound
That I should know your voice's churlish sound;
I know you have a far more milder tune
Than 'Peace, be quiet, wife;' but I have done.
Will ye go home? The door directs the way;
But, if you will not, my duty is to stay. (Exit.)[14] (I.i.105)

She does not even wait to see if he intends to leave, which in fact he does not. Porter also reminds us of the disruptive effects of shrewishness; the husbands and wives are in constant conflict, and a match between the children of the two families is in danger of being frustrated. But the personalities of the two women also produce some lively comedy. Throughout the play, in fact, Porter modulates between humour and seriousness so subtly that it is impossible to say where one ends and the other begins. Sometimes a comic speech is seen, on examination, to contain a few home truths that are to be accepted seriously; sometimes a serious speech reveals an undercurrent of wry humour. The style looks simple, but within it Porter achieves a delicate balance.

The play also raises the question of how a shrew is to be controlled. The pamphleteers, as we might expect, insist that the husband's reproofs should be administered tactfully and gently: 'And if he shall have occasion to speak sharply, and sometimes to reprove, he must beware that he do not the same in the presence of others; but let him keep his words until a convenient time (which is the point of a wise man) and then utter them in the spirit of meekness, and in the spirit of perfect love, and he must not let sometimes to cover faults, and wink at them, if they be not too great and intolerable.'[15] By the textbook

14 It is only fair to point out that Mistress Goursey's exit is not marked in the Quarto of 1599, but the dialogue between the two husbands, which follows immediately, clearly indicates that she has left the stage.
15 Cleaver, godlie forme, p. 164

standard, Barnes's conduct is absolutely correct; he does not lecture his wife as an underling, but advises her, kindly and gently, as his other self:

Wife, in my mind to-day you were to blame,
Although my patience did not blame ye for it:
Methought the rules of love and neighbourhood
Did not direct your thoughts; all indiscreet
Were your proceedings in the entertain
Of them that I invited to my house.
Nay, stay, I do not chide, but counsel, wife,
And in the mildest manner that I may:
You need not view me with a servant's eye,
Whose vassal senses tremble at the look
Of his displeased master. O my wife,
You are myself! When self sees fault in self,
Self is sin-obstinate, if self amend not ... (ii.i.p.114)

Goursey, on the other hand, in order to recover a letter his wife has snatched from him, falls into a spluttering rage. His broken, nearly incoherent speech is as far as it could possibly be from the smoothness and control of Barnes:

Shall I not have it? In troth, I'll try that:
Minion, I'll ha't; shall I not ha't? – I am loth –
Go to, take pausement, be advised –
In faith, I will; and stand not long upon it –
A woman of your years! I am ashamed
A couple of so long continuance
Should thus – God's foot – I cry God heart'ly mercy! –
Go to, ye vex me; and I'll vex ye for it;
Before I leave ye, I will make ye glad
To tender it on your knees; hear ye, I will, I will. (ii.iv.p.139)

The interesting point is that neither technique works. Barnes makes no headway at all, and Goursey earns only a temporary tactical withdrawal. The textbook view of marriage is amusingly exploded. The solution is finally given in dramatic terms, in a trick which forces the wives to relent: the husbands pretend to take the wives' accusations of adultery seriously, and prepare to fight each other. The wives, alarmed, are persuaded to withdraw their allegations and patch up the quarrel. Some flattening of the characters is involved, with the two couples acting in unison; this is characteristic of the last part of the play, which surrenders some of the early interest in character for the more conventional pleasures of an intricate plot. But in those early scenes, Porter's dramatization of the problems of marriage is both lively and telling.[16]

In Ben Jonson's treatment of the marriage problem, the emphasis is also on character, but on character as Jonson conceives it, comically distorted by folly. While other writers show the chaos a shrew creates in an entire family, Jonson focuses on the disruption of relations between husband and wife. In *Every Man out of his Humour* (Chamberlain's, 1599) Deliro is a cringing, servile husband who allows his wife Fallace to lord it over him. Having tasted power she guards it jealously, and the result is that they are both trapped on a treadmill of unhappiness and frustration: he is determined to please her, she is equally determined not to be pleased. He greets her with perfumes and she complains of the smell; he scatters flowers in her path and she abuses him for cutting them. The folly of this couple is amusing in a cold, sardonic way. And the explicit moral drawn by Macilente is equally cold:

> Husbands must take heed
> They give no gluts of kindness to their wives,
> But use them like their horses; whom they feed
> Not with a manger-full of meat together,
> But half a peck at once; and keep them so
> Still with an appetite to that they give them.
> He that desires to have a loving wife,
> Must bridle all the show of that desire:
> Be kind, not amorous; nor bewraying kindness,
> As if love wrought it, but considerate duty. (II.iv.63–72)

The brutality of the speech, treating marriage on a level with horse-keeping, is conditioned by the character of the speaker, a sour-tempered satirist. But it is also consistent with the spirit of icy contempt for folly that runs through the play. The insistence on order is familiar to us from other sources; but the harshness with which the consequences of disorder are shown is a product of Jonson's own satiric temperament, and Macilente's speech suggests that there are no gentle answers for human folly.

The same basic insight is given a more lively and expansive treatment in *Epicoene* (Queen's Revels, 1609), Jonson's comedy on the interrelated themes of marriage and noise. Here we see, even more vividly, the distortion of person-

---

16 Mistress Water-camlet, in *Anything for a Quiet Life*, is another shrew who is presented with a mixture of laughter and serious criticism, though here the comedy is broader and the blending is not so subtle. She too is brought to heel only by the threat of losing her husband.

ality which is both a cause and a product of disorder in marriage. The 'College' of ladies in this play is, among other things, an organized body of shrews who 'cry down, or up, what they like, or dislike ... with most masculine, or rather hermaphroditical authority' (I.i.78–80). In adopting this unnatural authority they have denied their own womanhood: among other things, they take mixtures to prevent childbirth: 'How should we maintain our youth and beauty else? Many births of a woman make her old, as many crops make the earth barren' (IV.iii.59–61). They prefer a parody of eternal youth, with the help of cosmetics, to accepting their natural roles as women. Jonson also shows, in the case of Tom Otter, the dislocation of a husband's nature when his wife takes over.[17] Otter married for money – 'I married with six thousand pound, I. I was in love with that' (IV.ii.78–9) – and he pays the price. Mistress Otter reminds him at one point of 'the instrument, when I married you ... That I would be Princess, and reign in mine own house: and you would be my subject, and obey me' (III.i.32–5). Not only has the inversion of the proper order been formalized; there is, in the terms 'Princess' and 'subject' something of a children's game of make-believe; the Otters, instead of living together like adults, have created a fantasy world for themselves.

Otter himself is particularly affected by this, reduced to childlike subservience and dependence, sometimes even treated like a domestic animal: 'By that light, I'll ha' you chain'd up, with your bull-dogs, and bear-dogs, if you be not civil the sooner. I'll send you to kennel, i'faith' (III.i.2–4). Treated like a child, he behaves like one, and retreats farther and farther from the adult world. Remembering fondly his old bear-baiting days, he calls his collection of cups by the names of animals, and plays with them as a child would. He pretends, for example, that a drinking contest is a fight between his bear, his bull, and his horse. There may be something Freudian in his fascination with cups; certainly he uses fantasy as a means of compensation for his wife's treatment of him, delivering long speeches of contempt for her when he thinks she is out of hearing: 'Wife! Buzz. *Titivilitium!* There's no such thing in nature. I confess, gentlemen, I have a cook, a laundress, a house-drudge, that serves my necessary turns, and goes under that title; but he's an ass that will be so uxorious, to tie his affections to one circle' (IV.ii.50–4). Mistress Otter is a conventional shrew, a lively but rather one-dimensional figure. But with her husband, Jonson has explored deeply the disruption that results in a husband's personality when he abdicates from his proper role.

The mirror image of this is the marriage of Morose and Epicoene, where the husband insists too much on his dominant role. He wants obedience in a wife,

---

17 See Edward B. Partridge, *The Broken Compass* (London, 1958), p. 168.

and for this reason, when Epicoene is offered to him, he considers even her poverty an advantage, since 'in respect of her poverty ... I shall have her more loving, and obedient' (II.v.92–3). When she tells him that she will leave even the selection of her wardrobe to him, he is delighted (II.v.76–86). Of course, his main reason for marrying her is her silence. In writings on marriage, this was considered to be woman's greatest virtue,[18] but Morose insists on it rather too much; this is part of his comic aversion to noise. Nor is this aversion merely a freak malady: it has a special comic significance. He announces, 'all discourses, but mine own, afflict me, they seem harsh, impertinent, and irksome' (II.i.4–5). According to John Palmer, 'the victim's dislike of noise – any noise, be it noted, except his own – is the physical expression of a sullen and unlovely disposition.'[19] And Edward B. Partridge suggests that 'Morose is comic, rather than psychopathic, because he is selfish and vain ... [He is] a proud, not a sick, man.'[20] Most important for our purposes, he wants a marriage he can dominate completely, a marriage in which he will do all the talking. His conception of the ideal relationship between himself and his wife is a gross, comic exaggeration of the proper one.

His punishment is significant, and highly amusing. No sooner is the marriage celebrated than Epicoene reveals herself as a woman with a will of her own and a very active tongue; she scorns any idea of marriage that would reduce her (as Morose intended) to a mere cipher: 'Why, did you think you had married a statue? or a motion, only? one of the French puppets, with the eyes turn'd with a wire? or some innocent out of the hospital, that would stand with her hands thus, and a plaise mouth, and look upon you?' (III.iv.37–41). Morose has married a wife who is the precise opposite of everything he wanted; it is a just and comic punishment for his ideas on marriage. He is, of course, desperately anxious to be rid of her, and ready to go to any lengths, even to gelding himself, in order to do so. When Dauphine offers him a way out, he is so grateful that he offers to make himself the young man's ward. Dauphine reveals that Epicoene is really a boy, and Morose is saved. Even this detail has, I think, a certain significance. The marriage that Morose made for himself was meant to satisfy a ludicrous demand; it is appropriate that it should turn out to be a mockery, a parody of marriage. In this case, as in the case of the Otters, the domineering partner has a de-natured spouse (though the plot circumstances are obviously quite different). And Jonson's ending is true to his satiric vision

18 See Robert Greene, *Penelope's Web* (London, 1587): 'Demaratus, an ambassador of Corinth, being demanded of Olimpias, Phillip's wife, how the ladies of his country behaved themselves, answered they were silent, comprehending under this word all other virtues' (sig.G²v).
19 *Ben Jonson* (London, 1934), p. 181
20 *Broken Compass*, p. 171

of marriage: most comedies conclude with a wedding; the happy ending of *Epicoene* is a divorce.

But Jonson's satiric vision is uncommon, and most comedies achieve a happy ending for the couple somehow, even if (as in *Anything for a Quiet Life*) they have to force it. The ending imposed by a plot device is common enough, but there are other plays which give the problem of adjustment in marriage a more searching consideration. They do so, however, in dramatic terms. A dramatist is not (formally at least) a marriage counsellor. If he were, we could expect to hear this sort of thing from him:

Knowing once a couple which were both choleric, and yet never fell out, I asked the man how they did order the matter, that their infirmity did not make them discord. He answered me, when her fit is upon her I yield to her, as Abraham did to Sara; and when my fit is upon me, she yields to me, and so we never strive together, but asunder. Methought it was a good example to commend unto all married folks; for everyone hath his frenzy and loveth them that can bear his infirmity.[21]

What happened when the fit was on both of them at once the writer does not tell us. The point is that conflict as a means of reaching an understanding is ruled out, and this view is characteristic of contemporary marriage tracts. But for a dramatist, and particularly a comic dramatist, conflict within marriage has a positive theatrical value, as a source of lively and amusing scenes. And more than that, it can be seen as the medium through which a couple can reach an understanding. There is an element of battle in love-making that the moralists might not be prepared to admit, but that imaginative writers have always acknowledged.

The case is explicitly argued – with an agreeable mixture of sermonizing and theatrical fireworks – by Thomas Dekker in the two parts of *The Honest Whore* (Prince Henry's, 1604 and *c.* 1605), the first part written in collaboration with Middleton. Dekker presents the two marriages, one in each play, of the patient linen-draper Candido. We see him in Part One coping with his shrewish wife Viola, ignoring her brazen and deliberate offences with the miraculous patience that has made him famous throughout his city:

CANDIDO
Here wife, begin you to the gentleman.
WIFE
I begin to him? (*Casts down the drink*)

---

21 Henry Smith, *A Preparatiue to Mariage*, in *The Sermons of Maister Henrie Smith, gathered into one volume* (London, 1593), p. 39

CANDIDO
George, fill't up again;
'Twas my fault, my hand shook. (I.v.137–9)

Candido defends his patience as 'the honey 'gainst a waspish wife' (v.ii.509). The marriage counsellors would agree. But Viola holds different views on the subject: Candido's patience worries her: 'I have heard it often said, that he who cannot be angry, is no man' (I.ii.63–4). She yearns for a little conflict, for a dash of anger from him. One suspects that she wants to be dominated, that her 'longing,' which she appears not to understand herself, is the expression of a deep psychological need: 'I protest to thee Fustigo, I love him most affection-ately, but I know not – I ha' such a tickling within me – such a strange longing; nay, verily I do long ... I long to have my patient husband eat up a whole por-cupine, to the intent, the bristling quills may stick about his lips like a Flemish mustacho, and be shot at me; I shall be leaner than the new moon, unless I can make him horn mad' (I.ii.80–2,87–91). When she has him locked up in Bedlam, however, she realizes that she has gone too far. She misses him, and wants him back, on his own terms if necessary; like Porter's shrews she is brought round by the threat of losing her husband altogether; but the feeling persists, as it does in *Two Angry Women*, that this is a solution based on a plot device rather than one springing from the wife's character: her 'longing' disappears a little too easily.

Candido has won the battle by passive resistance, but there are lingering doubts; and the Duke, at the end of the play, though he is deeply impressed by Candido's patience, takes up in a quieter way the reservations that Viola had expressed earlier: ''Twere sin all women should such husbands have, / For every man must then be his wife's slave' (v.ii.512–13). This is more than just a joke in passing: it indicates a doubt so serious that the issue has to be taken up in Part Two. Candido's view of marriage, as expressed in Part One, demands harmony, and sees this harmony as the natural solution for all marital disputes:

Pray wear a peaceful temper, be my wife,
That is, be patient; for a wife and husband
Share but one soul between them; this being known,
Why should not one soul then agree in one? (I.v.197–200)

This is part of the conventional formula for a perfect marriage; but only part of it. Candido ignores the husband's responsibility to rule.

This view is put to him forcibly by the knight Lodovico at the opening of Part Two. Candido has married a second wife, who is turning out to be another shrew: 'Will you be a tame pigeon still? Shall your back be like a tortoise-shell, to let carts go over it, yet not break? ... you know, that a woman was made of the rib of a man, and that rib was crooked. The moral of which is, that a man must from the beginning be crooked to his wife; be you like an orange to her, let her cut you never so fair, be you sour as vinegar; will you be ruled by me?' (I.iii.104–15). He adds that he does not mean brutality, but simply firmness: 'I do not bid you beat her, nor give her black eyes, nor pinch her sides; but cross her humours' (II.ii.30–1). Candido cannot be genuinely impatient; but, urged on by Lodovico, he agrees to simulate wrath in order to keep his new wife under control:

A curst cow's milk I ha' drunk once before,
And 'twas so rank in taste, I'll drink no more.
Wife, I'll tame you. (II.ii.72–4)

She accepts the challenge. The battle is conducted on the level of slapstick, with symbolic overtones: they prepare to fence, he with a yard and she with an ell. 'Yard' being a common term for the male sex organ, its use here suggests an elemental sexual conflict. She demands the right to strike the first blow, he grants it – and she kneels:

Behold, I am such a cunning fencer grown,
I keep my ground, yet down I will be thrown
With the least blow you give me; I disdain
The wife that is her husband's sovereign.
She that upon your pillow first did rest,
They say, the breeches wore, which I detest:
The tax which she imposed upon you, I abate you,
If me you make your master, I shall hate you.
The world shall judge who offers fairest play;
You win the breeches, but I win the day. (II.ii.106–115)

Conflict has become a means of understanding between husband and wife. Candido learns that patience must be tempered with authority, and that this is what women want.

The battle of the sexes becomes literally that in Fletcher's reply to *The Taming of the Shrew*, *The Woman's Prize, or The Tamer Tamed* (auspices unknown, *c.* 1611). The marriage of Petruchio and Maria was an arranged match, though not an enforced one, and the couple have to work out an understanding for themselves after the wedding. This is particularly important in view of the failure of Petruchio's first marriage. His first wife was a shrew, and he tried to handle her simply by bullying her. Everything we hear about this marriage (and constant references keep it in our minds throughout the play) indicates that it brought no joy to either partner. Petruchio himself admits,

Had I not ev'ry morning a rare breakfast,
Mixt with a learned lecture of ill language,
Louder than Tom o' Lincoln; and at dinner,
A diet of the same dish? Was there evening
That e'er past over us, without 'thou knave,'
Or 'thou whore,' for digestion? Had I ever
A pull at this same poor sport men run mad for,
But like a cur I was fain to show my teeth first,
And almost worry her? (III.iii.157–65)

Other characters, recalling Petruchio's method of dealing with his first wife, predict that Maria will be treated as a slave:

She must do nothing of herself; not eat,
Drink, say, sir, how do ye? make her ready, piss,
Unless he bid her. (I.i.45–7)

But Maria is quite capable of looking after herself. She has her own views on marriage, which are opposed to the idea that a wife is a slave who must be beaten into dumb submission. Fellowship and equality are the principles on which she insists:

By the faith I have
In mine own noble will, that childish woman
That lives a prisoner to her husband's pleasure
Has lost her making, and becomes a beast,
Created for his use, not fellowship. (I.ii.136–40)

Tell me of due obedience? What's a husband?
What are we married for, to carry sumpters?
Are we not one piece with you, and as worthy
Our own intentions, as you yours? (III.iii.97–100)

She makes it clear, too, that her crusade is not simply a personal one, but an important point of female honour, seen in a broad context. Her failure would be a failure for all womankind, and she begs to be punished for failure by having the most important function of her womanhood destroyed:

> _Stay: Lucina hear me,
> Never unlock the treasure of my womb
> For humane fruit, to make it capable;
> Nor never with thy secret hand make brief
> A mother's labour to me, if I do
> Give way unto my married husband's will,
> Or be a wife, in anything but hopes,
> Till I have made him easy as a child,
> And tame as fear. (1.ii.107–15)

This invocation is serious, even impressive, and it helps to provide an anchor of earnestness for the mock-heroics that follow. The rebellion is seen in the widest context of human history. Maria's comrade-in-arms Bianca invokes the past:

> All the several wrongs
> Done by imperious husbands to their wives
> These thousand years and upwards, strengthen thee:
> Thou hast a brave cause. (1.ii.122–5)

And Maria herself looks to the future:

> My rest is up wench, and I pull for that
> Will make me ever famous. They that lay
> Foundations, are half builders, all men say. (1.ii.192–4)

This comic inflation does not have the effect of mocking the women's enterprise. It is, rather, conscious wit on the part of the characters, and their zest is infectious.

The same effect is produced by the mock-military tone of the first stage of Maria's conquest of Petruchio, in which Fletcher seems to be recalling *Lysistrata*. The battle of the sexes has become a battle indeed. On the wedding night, Maria refuses to go to bed with her new husband, and she and Bianca lock themselves in. Their chamber quickly takes on the attributes of a besieged city. As one of Petruchio's friends describes it,

> The chamber's nothing but a mere Ostend,
> In every window pewter cannons mounted,
> You'll quickly find with what they are charg'd, sir. (1.iii.88–90)

Bianca draws several parallels with the siege of Troy, and the affair actually does take on the scale of a comic epic when a drunken and disorderly Army of Women marches to the relief of the besieged chamber. Fletcher here touches a strain of comic fantasy that he never quite recaptures in the later scenes. Petruchio's effort to come to terms with his wife is quite literally the parleying of an attacking commander with the garrison of a fortress, and the fortress surrenders only on terms highly advantageous to itself. There is splendid fun in the transformation of an ordinary bedroom into a besieged city, and the Army of Women – tipsy, belligerent, and singing ribald songs about the day when the women shall wear the breeches – is a delight. Throughout the fun, however, we never lose sight of Maria's purposes, and the military comedy is both engaging in itself, and an amusing way of putting across the play's main point.

When the army has marched away, Petruchio and Maria are left to settle the affair between them, and the duel is kept theatrically vital by the wit of both parties. Maria, as the party with the initiative, has greater opportunities for comic invention, whether it is locking her husband up as a plague victim, or, when he threatens to leave the country, calling his bluff and giving him a mock-heroic send-off:

Go, worthy man, and bring home understanding.
...
For if the merchant through unknown seas plough
To get his wealth, then dear sir, what must you
To gather wisdom? Go, and go alone,
Only your noble mind for your companion,
And if a woman may win credit with you,
Go far; too far you cannot; still the farther
The more experience finds you. (IV.v.153–61)

Petruchio has his opportunities too, generally for expressing exasperation:

She hath neither manners, honesty, behaviour,
Wife-hood, nor woman-hood, nor any moral
Can force me to think she had a mother. (IV.v.107–9)

Whatever their differences on marriage are, Petruchio and Maria have wit and liveliness in common, and each can appreciate these qualities in the other. This is the basis of a mutual affection of which we are given continual glimpses throughout the play. After one of her tricks, he remarks,

Now if she have a colour, for the fault is
A cleanly one, upon my conscience

I shall forgive her yet, and find a something
Certain, I married her for: her wit. (iv.ii.23–6)

She returns his affection, and admits as much:

>   were I yet unmarried, free to choose
> Through all the tribes of man, I'd take Petruchio
> In's shirt, with one ten groats to pay the priest,
> Before the best man living, or the ablest
> That e'er leap'd out of Lancashire, and they are right ones. (i.iii.152–6)

This is the paradox of their relationship: a quarrel stubbornly maintained on both sides by two people who freely admit that they are fond of each other. Petruchio, not being the one who started the quarrel, and not grasping its purpose, asks her to explain herself:

PETRUCHIO
Death, this is a riddle:
I love you, and I love you not.
MARIA
It is so:
And till your own experience do untie it,
This distance I must keep. (i.iii.165–8)

This exchange is the key to the play, as I see it. Maria cannot give way to affection until she has purged Petruchio of his bullying tendencies. This she must do by employing his own methods, the only ones he would understand, and by using against him the wit and vitality for which he loves her. She recognizes · that love is not a sufficient basis for a happy marriage unless it is accompanied by a proper understanding of a wife's relationship to her husband, and she recognizes further that, Petruchio being the sort of man he is, this point can best be made by shock treatment.

Once every device he has tried to bring her to meekness – including shamming death – has failed, she herself capitulates. Having established her ascendancy over him, she retreats into the subservient position proper to a wife:

I have done my worst, and have my end, forgive me;
From this hour make me what you please: I have tam'd ye,
And am now vow'd your servant: look not strangely,
Nor fear what I say to you. Dare you kiss me?
Thus I begin my new love. (v.iv.44–8)

We should be careful how we interpret Maria's submission. The important point is that it is a voluntary one, made only after she has established that she can, of her own ability, lead her husband by the nose if she wants to. The conclusion is, I think, that men and women are potentially equal and that woman submits in marriage not because she is inherently baser than her husband, but because she chooses, for the sake of order, to be obedient. Consequently, no man should presume too much on his right to give orders or think that, because his wife obeys him, she is an inferior being. Fletcher's gift for witty dialogue and for zany fantasy ensures that his presentation of the battle of the sexes is charming and amusing; but the lightness of treatment does not detract from a serious and attractive belief in the power of the age-old debate to create a firm union, based on love, mutual knowledge, and respect, between the man and woman involved.

In *The Shoemakers' Holiday* (Admiral's, 1599) Dekker portrays a happy marriage in action, in terms that the moralists would find a little shocking. The household of Simon Eyre and his wife is one continual uproar. Eyre refers to his wife at various times as 'this wench with the mealy mouth that will never tire' (1.i.127–8), 'kitchen-stuff,' and 'brown bread tannakin' (11.iii.59). When she tells him to be careful what he says to the king, he exerts his authority over her with some dazzling insults: 'Away you Islington whitepot, hence you happerarse, you barley pudding full of maggots, you broil'd carbonado, avaunt, avaunt, avoid Mephistophilis; shall Sim Eyre learn to speak of you, Lady Madgie? Vanish Mother Miniver Cap, vanish, go, trip and go, meddle with your partlets, and your pishery pashery, your flues and your whirligigs, go, rub, out of mine alley' (v.iv.46–51). Mistress Eyre cannot quite come up to this standard, but she is capable of holding her own. There is never any malice in this verbal brawling; it is simply the overflow of high spirits. Behind all the shouting and abuse one can detect a rough but solid affection, which comes to the surface occasionally. When Eyre dons the alderman's gown, for example, his wife is delighted with him, and there is an attractive warmth in their exchange:

EYRE
How say'st thou Maggie, am I not brisk? Am I not fine?
WIFE
Fine? By my troth sweet heart very fine; by my troth I never lik'd thee so well in my life sweet heart. But let that pass, I warrant there be many women in the city have not such handsome husbands, but only for their apparel, but let that pass too. (11.iii.110–14)

When he presents her to the king, he makes it clear that their marriage, after many years, is still very much alive: 'Mark this old wench, my king, I danc'd the shaking of the sheets with her six and thirty years ago, and yet I hope to get two or three young Lord Mayors ere I die' (v.v.27–30). Beside this, the model marriages described in the pamphlets, all patience and gentleness, look pale and theoretical.

The plays examined in this chapter show comedy's ability to question its own premises. Marriage, so often taken for granted as a structural device, is here examined, with some very lively results. Often the formula for a successful marriage turns out to be just one more plot convention, and Jonson's sardonic view of the institution is not encouraging, to say the least. But, in their different ways, Fletcher and Dekker see in the abrasiveness of a really noisy marriage an unorthodox but valuable formula for wedlock, and their marriage-comedies are both lively and humane. We are allowed to enjoy the comedy of the conflict, the disruption of conventional harmony; yet at the same time, paradoxically, the conflict is itself a means of cementing the underlying social order.

6
Chaste maids and whores

MALHEUREUX
This lust is a most deadly sin, sure.
FREEVILL
Nay, 'tis a most lively sin, sure.
Marston, *The Dutch Courtesan*

If Elizabethan attitudes on marriage were subtly balanced, poised between severity and liberality, attitudes to sexual behaviour were – publicly, at least – absolute. Chastity is woman's natural state – so much so that 'if a woman perish in the water, she swims with her face downward.'[1] A single moment can tip the scales between virtue and disgrace, and the loss is irrecoverable. Robert Greene writes of a 'store of balm which could cure strange wounds, only not that wound which women receive when they lose their maidenheads, for no herb hath virtue enough to scrape out that blot and therefore it is the greater blemish.'[2] When a woman falls her whole nature is corrupted: the word 'whore' is conventionally used for a woman who has slipped once. And the professional whore becomes, in popular writings, a stock figure of evil. She is always physically grotesque,[3] and it is conventionally assumed that her wickedness is not

---

1 Thomas Heywood, *A Curtaine Lectvre ...* (London, 1638), p. 4
2 *A Qvip for an Vpstart Courtier* (London, 1592), sig.B³r
3 Francis Lenton, in *Characterismi* (London, 1631), describes 'an old bawd' as 'a menstruous beast, engendered of divers most filthy excrements, by the stench of whose breath the air is so infected, that her presence is an inevitable contagion, her eyes more poisonous than the basilisk; her nose (if any) most pestilently pocky, her tongue more subtle than the hyena, who still howls in some feigned voice for the devouring of innocents, one who hath damnably destroyed her own soul, and is devilishly devising the destruction of others ... Diseases at last dry up her marrow, and rottenness so shivers her, that she drops asunder on a sudden, and

confined to the bedroom, but that she is ripe for any sort of crime: 'She is the very compendium and abstract of all baseness, nor is there any abomination to which she is unapt ... Lust and murder are her professions, and she cares not who knows it.'[4]

This absolute, black-and-white attitude is reflected straightforwardly in many comedies of the period. The chaste maid becomes a convenient stock type, one half of a simple confrontation between virtue and vice. Kate Worldly, in Nathan Field's *A Woman is a Weather-cock* (Queen's Revels, *c.* 1609) – a play which is not nearly so anti-feminist as its title suggests – is slandered at the church door on the day of her wedding, and refuses to sleep with her husband until he has righted her honour by killing the slanderer in a duel. Her reputation for chastity is so important that it must be preserved by drastic measures. Meg Overreach, in Massinger's *A New Way to Pay Old Debts* (Red Bull Company? 1621) rejects her father's suggestion that she should prostitute herself to Lord Lovell as a means of furthering the match between them. She speaks in terms of absolutes, of heaven and hell, and insists that one act of sin would make her totally worthless:

> Though you could dispense
> With your own honour; cast aside religion,
> The hopes of heaven, or fear of hell, excuse me,
> In worldly policy, this is not the way
> To make me his wife, his whore I grant it may do.
> My maiden honour so soon yielded up,
> Nay prostituted, cannot but assure him
> I that am light to him will not hold weight
> When his, tempted by others: so in judgement
> When to his lust I have given up my honour
> He must, and will forsake me. (III.ii.129–39)

Similarly, in the anonymous *The Fair Maid of the Exchange* (auspices unknown, *c.* 1602), Phyllis thanks the man who has saved her and her companion from rape: 'Thanks, honest friend, who from the gates of death / Hath set our virgin souls at liberty' (ll.103–4). This is not just a flourish; it indicates the character's deep obsession with her chastity. Later in the play, when a man compliments her on her figure, the same obsession makes her attack him in terms which seem out of all proportion to the offence:

What am I, you, cipher, parenthesis of words,

wretchedly dies without pity; for whom, a Christian burial is too courteous.' (sigs. C³r-⁴v).
4 Lenton, *Characterismi*, sigs.E⁶r-v

Stall-troubler, prater, what sit I here for nought?
Bestow your lustful courtships on your minions,
This place holds none; you and your companion,
Get you down the stairs, or I protest
I'll make this squared walk too hot for you. (ll.1261–6)

The incongruity is revealing: Phyllis's devotion to her chastity is so absolute
that she cannot treat even a trifling offence mildly. Flirtation or attempted rape
– each meets the full blaze of her anger. Nor is she untypical. A strong-minded
woman driving off a seducer is one of the most frequently recurring situations
in citizen comedy, though this play is a little unusual in the aggressive wit the
women (Phyllis is not the only one) display. Very often, as in this play, the
setting is a shop, with the woman behind the counter, and the dialogue plays
with the ideas of buying and selling; since the seducer is often of a higher rank
than the shopgirl, the setting makes the scene a compliment to the chastity of
middle-class women.[5] There is always something a little mechanical about such
scenes, with the chaste maid and the seducer going through set motions, like
wind-up toys.

Equally predictable is the stock type of the vicious whore. In moralizing prodigal plays, she is a convenient instrument for tempting and then chastising the
prodigal. In Cooke's *Greene's Tu Quoque* (Queen Anne's, 1611) the prodigal
Spendall is preyed upon by Sweatman, a bawd, and Tickleman, a whore. While
he has money, they cadge from him unashamedly, professing great affection
for him. But when the money runs out, and he comes to them for help to avoid
imprisonment for debt, Tickleman's reaction is just what we might expect:

Why, you impudent rogue, do you come to me for money?
Or do I know you? What acquaintance, pray,
Hath ever pass'd betwixt yourself and me? (p. 245)

Even cooler is the sanctimonious pose that Sweatman strikes:

Pray, carry him to prison, let him smart for't;
Perhaps 'twill tame the wildness of his youth,
And teach him how to lead a better life.
He had good counsel here, I can assure you,
And if he would have took it. (p. 246)

---

5 See also Dekker's *The Shoemakers' Holiday* (Admiral's, 1599), Heywood's *The Wise-woman
of Hogsdon* (Queen Anne's, c. 1604), and Cooke's *Greene's Tu Quoque* (Queen Anne's, 1611).
Though the auspices of *The Fair Maid of the Exchange* are unknown, the other plays mentioned
all belong to the public theatres, with their tradition of moralizing comedy.

The hypocrisy is amusing in its sheer brazen impudence. Behind the comedy, however, lies a fairly serious awareness that a whore builds her life on false-hood, moving from one hypocritical pose to another, with selfishness as her only real motive.

In the anonymous *How a Man May Choose a Good Wife from a Bad* (Worcester's, *c.* 1602) the whore's distorted values are set forth more explicitly. Mary's defence of her trade is something more interesting than a simple statement of immorality: it is a parody of goodness. Kisses and oaths, love and suffering: all these are perverted by her:

She that with kisses can both kill and cure,
That lives by love, that swears by nothing else
But by a kiss, which is no common oath;
That lives by lying, and yet oft tells truth;
That takes most pleasure when she takes most pains;
She's a good wench, my boy, and so am I. (ii.iii.p.36)

The paradoxes and the riddling ambiguity indicate the duplicity of the character's nature. The suppression of human values in favour of money, on which the whore bases her life, is displayed in a speech by Mary's mentor, a bawd with the gruesomely appropriate name of Mistress Splay:

Money can make a slavering tongue speak plain.
If he that loves thee be deform'd and rich,
Accept his love: gold hides deformity.
Gold can make limping Vulcan walk upright;
Make squint eyes straight, a crabbed face look smooth,
Gilds copper noses, makes them look like gold;
Fills age's wrinkles up, and makes a face,
As old as Nestor's, look as young as Cupid's. (ii.iii.p.37)

Young Arthur, obsessed with Mary's charm, poisons his wife in order to marry the whore (or so he thinks; the poison, since this is a comedy, is a harmless sleeping draught). Mary, when she hears of the murder, immediately reveals it in the hope that she will inherit Arthur's money after he has been executed. This is the logical extension of her duplicity and greed; she pretends love to Arthur, but in reality she will use even his life to get money for herself. The plot of *How a Man May Choose a Good Wife from a Bad* became a standard one: we see it repeated in its essentials in *The Fair Maid of Bristow*, *The Dutch Courtesan*, and *The Fleer* (all of which will be discussed later), and there are analogues with other plays.[6] Its presentation of the whore, on which the plot largely depends, is also standard. Obsessed with money, she will suppress or even pervert human values; in this way, she resembles the usurer, and like him she is often presented as a satiric caricature. This is perhaps the reason why, in *A Trick to Catch the Old One* and *Ram Alley*, the usurer is punished by marriage to a whore; one feels they deserve each other. In the anonymous *The Fair Maid of Bristow* (King's, *c.* 1604) the caricature is taken to the point at which Florence, the whore of the piece, threatens a man with death simply for telling the truth about her:

FLORENCE
Call'st thou me whore? Now by this light
I'll have thee murd'red, and if gold can do it.
BLUNT
Gold can do much, but devil can do more,
Here is a true pattern, of a common whore. (III.iii.521–4)

The whore's concern for maintaining false appearances cannot go much farther than this; but Blunt's comment indicates that we are meant to take this extreme behaviour as typical.

So far, what we have seen is conventional drama reflecting conventional morality. But there is also such a thing as conventional immorality. Where sexual attitudes are austere, joking about sex naturally flourishes as a safety-valve, and the bawdy humour which accepts sex as a laughing matter becomes in itself conventional. Comedies which present whores with indulgent amusement are at least as common as the moralizing type, and just as predictable. What is interesting is that the jokes and the sermons share the same analysis of the whore's way of life. To buy and sell the act of love is not just vicious but inherently absurd, and the union of money and sex, which we saw in Mistress Splay's speech, is not just unnatural but comically incongruous. Just as (in *The Staple of News*, for example) a usurer is a bawd to money, a prostitute is a merchant of sex, and the absurdity provides easy material for jokes, the pun on 'wholesale' being especially popular.[7] Furthermore, the duplicity of the whore (who spends her working hours acting a lie) can easily be dramatized as amusing

---

6 See Arthur Hobson Quinn, Introduction to his edition of *The Fair Maid of Bristow* (Philadelphia, 1902), pp. 11–14 and p. 29; and C.R. Baskervill, 'Sources and Analogues of *How a Man May Choose a Good Wife from a Bad*,' *PMLA*, xxiv, New Series xvii (December 1909), 711–30.
7 Cf. Marston, *The Dutch Courtesan*, I.ii.38–9; and Middleton, *Michaelmas Term*, IV.ii.15

chicanery. The whore's posture of respectability leads just as easily to laughter as to moral outrage.

Doll, in Dekker and Webster's *Northward Ho* (Paul's, 1605), offers a defence of her trade (such defences are, in fact, a recurring convention)[8] in which the connection between prostitution and commerce is played upon for comic effect: 'Silver is the King's stamp, man God's stamp, and a woman is man's stamp, we are not current till we pass from one man to another' (I.ii.81–3). Her pose of respectability is amusing, and it works so well that it wins her a rich marriage at the end of the play. The pose is carried even further by Mistress Correction, the old bawd in Edward Sharpham's *Cupid's Whirligig* (King's Revels, 1607), who prides herself on being a high-class tradeswoman with a select clientele: 'I have pensioners, and gentlemen ushers, knights, captains, and commanders, lieutenants, and ancients, voluntary gentlemen, aye, and men that wear their cloaks lined through with velvet; I entertain no mutton-eating Inns-a-court men, no half-lined-cloak citizens, nor flat-capp'd prentices, no, the best come to my house' (sig.C⁴v). She says of one of her employees: 'Truly sir a very courteous gentlewoman, and she loves to act in as clean linen as any gentlewoman of her function about the town' (sig. C⁴v). The old bawd's insistence on the proprieties is presented as a humorous quirk of character, and we accept it as such.[9] In the second part of Heywood's *If You Know Not Me, You Know Nobody* (Queen Anne's, 1605), the scene with Jack and Old Hobson in the brothel is full of jokes about 'ware' and 'commodities' (pp.307–12), and there is another ramification of the whore's pretence of respectability when the Puritan Timothy Thin-beard describes prostitutes as though they were a religious sect: 'I was bound for France, landed in France, dispatch'd some secret business for a sister in France, and from her have French tokens to deliver to the sisterhood whom I shall first encounter in England' (p.305).[10] The *double entendre* makes even the pox a laughing matter. This, by the way, is the only case under discussion of a public theatre play which allows this kind of joking about prostitution; it tends to be a specialty of the private theatres, while the adult companies take the more serious view that we have seen in *How a Man May Choose*

---

8 We shall notice them in *Michaelmas Term*, *The Fleer*, and *The Dutch Courtesan*, all of which are discussed later in the chapter. In every case the connection between sex and commerce is the basis of the humour.

9 In Dekker and Webster's *Westward Ho* (Paul's, 1604), Birdlime, a similar character, gives herself amusingly sanctimonious airs: 'there's a difference between a cogging bawd and an honest motherly gentlewoman' (II.ii.20–1).

10 The joking connection between prostitution and Puritanism, which can probably be taken as a comment on the hypocrisy of both parties, is also made in *The Dutch Courtesan*, in which Mary Faugh describes herself as 'one of the Family of Love' (I.ii.17) and adds, 'I trust I am none of the wicked that eat fish o'Fridays' (I.ii.19).

and *The Fair Maid of Bristow*.[11] Even the whore's lack of loyalty, a serious matter in the prodigal plays, becomes a joke in Dekker and Webster's *Westward Ho* (Paul's, 1604). Tenterhook creeps up behind the punk Luce, puts his hands over her eyes, and asks her to guess who it is. She goes through quite a long list of her customers without coming to the right answer (IV.i.58–67).[12]

In Middleton's *Your Five Gallants* (Queen's Revels, c. 1605) a brace of whores take a prominent part in the action. Middleton does not sentimentalize them: they are as cynical and deceptive as the strumpets of a moral prodigal comedy; but the dramatic attitude towards them is, for the most part, one of amused indulgence. Primero, the bawd-gallant, comments on their promiscuity, but he sees it not as treachery, but as the sign of an agreeable and biddable nature:

> the prettiest kind of fowl;
> So tame, so gentle, e'en to strangers' hands
> So soon familiar; suffer to be touch'd
> Of those they ne'er saw twice: the dove's not like 'em. (I.i.138–41)

The cunning with which he turns a vice into a virtue rouses laughter, and disarms conventional criticism. The deceptiveness of the trade is conveyed in a sequence in which Primero and his courtesans make an elaborate pretence at being a music-school. This is the occasion for some bawdy quibbling:

> And I may safely swear they practis'd music;
> They're natural at prick-song.
> ...
> You shall have 'em sometimes in every corner of the house, with their viols between their legs, and play the sweetest strokes. (II.i.44–5, 75–7)

The *double entendre* is also a sly acknowledgment that their respectability is only a pose. The masquerade is comic in itself, for not only do the courtesans

---

11 A general fondness for *double entendre*, however, cuts across repertory barriers. *The Shoemakers' Holiday*, for example, is full of bawdy innuendo about pricks, awls, entering, standing stiffly, and so forth (especially I.i.136–60). Even the writers of moral tracts cannot always resist the temptation. Nicholas Breton, in *The Good and the Badde* (London, 1616), remarks, in the midst of a tirade against a bawd, that 'she is partly a surgeon, but mostly for the allaying of swellings in the lower parts, and hath commonly a charm to conjure the devil into hell' (p. 32).

12 The same joke occurs in an anecdote related by one of the characters in *How a Man May Choose* (III.ii.43–4), though the context of that play makes its implications a little more serious. Versions of this joke are still current.

pretend to be sanctimonious, but by their agility in detecting any bawdy reference, they satirize the sort of women they are impersonating:

PRIMERO
They blush at their very lessons; they'll not endure
To hear of a stop, a prick, or a semiquaver.
FIRST COURTESAN
O, out upon you!
PRIMERO
La, I tell you; – you'll bear me witness, gentlemen,
If their complaints come to their parents' ears,
They're words of art I teach 'em, nought but art.
GOLDSTONE
Why, 'tis most certain.
BUNGLER
For all the scholars know that *musica est ars*.
ALL THE COURTESANS
O beastly word! (ii.i.91–9)

The courtesans do not merely imitate respectability; they parody it, and score
a comic point in doing so. Their deception, like the tricks of *The Alchemist*, is
a joke they share with the audience.

Sexual morality, then, is a matter that evokes stock responses, expressed in
stock dramatic conventions, in a large number of plays. The opposing figures
of chaste maid and whore may be lively, but in most cases they are not examined
in depth or in detail. And the tenacity of the conventions is indicated by the
fact that many of the attempts to treat them differently are uncertainly handled.
This is true, for example, of two plays which appear to challenge the idea that
an unmarried woman must be either a virgin or a whore. Since the late Victorian
period, this idea has crumbled so thoroughly before the assaults of novelists and
playwrights that it no longer seems worth attacking, but it meets with only feeble opposition in Jacobean comedy. In Middleton's *The Family of Love* (Admiral's? c. 1602) the moral position of Gerardine and Maria, who sleep
together before their wedding, is ambiguous. At the beginning of the play,
Gerardine is placed in opposition to the cynical, lecherous gallants Lipsalve and
Gudgeon, whom he addresses as 'You libertines, who never knew the joys /
Nor precious thoughts of two consenting hearts' (i.ii.16–17). He speaks of the
purity of love: 'My love's chaste smile to all the world doth speak / Her spotless
innocence' (i.ii.155–6). And Maria speaks of the value of 'honour'd nuptials and
a regular life' (ii.iv.13). It is therefore something of a shock to find Gerardine
seducing Maria, with a cynical bawdry that recalls Lipsalve and Gudgeon:

MARIA
You break all modest bounds; away, away!
GERARDINE
So when men come behind do women say.
MARIA
Come, come, I say –
GERARDINE
     Ay, that's the word indeed:
Men that come bold before are like to speed. (III.i.56–9)

At this point Gerardine's demands seem to be presented as thoroughly immoral. Yet after Maria has yielded, the tone changes once more, and we are asked to regard what the lovers have done as justified, partly by love itself, and partly as a way of forcing Maria's guardian to consent to their marriage:

MARIA
     ... Thy earnest, then, of love,
Ere Sol have compass'd half the signs, I fear
Will show a blushing fault; but 'twas thine aim
T'enforce consent in him that bars thy claim.
GERARDINE
Love salves that fault: let time our guilt reveal,
I'll ne'er deny my deed, my hand, and seal. (III.vii.13–18)

They still use the words 'fault' and 'guilt,' but the tone is calm and confident; instead of remorse, there is a sense that love may override the demands of strict morality. This justification, however, is not invoked until we have been treated to what looks like a thoroughly improper seduction scene, and one suspects either moral confusion, or deliberate titillation.[13]

 There is a similar ambiguity in the Jane Russell subplot of Middleton and Rowley's *A Fair Quarrel* (Prince's, *c.* 1617), generally assigned to Rowley. Jane and Fitzallen seem to have undertaken, in secret, a marriage contract, which has not yet been confirmed by a church ceremony. They have consummated their union, and Jane is pregnant. According to the Church, such consummation, coming before the church service, is sinful and immoral, though

---

13 If one were to accept Gerard J. Eberle's interesting and carefully presented case for Dekker's participation in the play, 'Dekker's Part in *The Familie of Love*,' *Joseph Quincy Adams Memorial Studies*, ed. James G. McManaway *et al.* (Washington, D.C., 1948), pp. 723–38, the inconsistency might be accounted for by a breakdown in collaboration; but we have enough evidence from Middleton's unaided work to suggest that he was capable of creating his own moral ambiguities, and even confusions, without interference from another writer.

the contract itself is a legal marriage.[14] The author exploits the ambiguity of the situation: Jane behaves as though she expects to become a figure of scandal if the child's birth is revealed, and she continually uses language suggesting guilt – ''twas love did sin' (II.ii.64); 'I'm the bad mother, – if it be offence' (III.ii.23). Yet the fact that they are contracted is used to sanction the birth of the child at the end of the play. Fitzallen says

Nor is it basely bred, as you imagine,
For we were wedded by the hand of heaven
Ere this work was begun. (v.i.371–3)

One suspects the author of titillation; like Middleton in *The Family of Love* he is trying to have both the sin and the sanction.

In these plays the absolute attitude to chastity is still, in the last analysis, assumed, and the audience is evidently expected to relish the ambiguity of the lovers' situation in relation to the code. A less ambiguous treatment is found in the anonymous *Wily Beguiled* (Paul's? *c*. 1602). The lovers Lelia and Sophos are forced to flee Lelia's home to prevent her father from marrying her to some-one else. Once they are on their own, Sophos proposes, 'Then let us solace, and in love's delight, / And sweet embracings spend the live-long night' (ll.2179–80). There is no moral questioning, or even an attempt at justification. The consummation of their love is simply accepted as the natural thing to do; and, because no fuss is made about it, it becomes dramatically acceptable as well. The treatment of the subject in this play, though it is little more than a touch in passing, is more honest and attractive than the calculated ambiguity of *A Fair Quarrel* and *The Family of Love*.

Of course a dramatist can always get special effects through the deliberate reversal of a stereotype, and in a couple of cases this is done with the stock figure of the treacherous whore. In Middleton's *A Trick to Catch the Old One* (Paul's, *c*. 1605) and Barry's *Ram Alley* (King's Revels, *c*. 1608), the whore is depicted as a good wench, with no real harm in her, and the stock charge of disloyalty is repudiated. The courtesan is loyal to the prodigal, and joins him in his attempt to win back his estate. In Middleton's play, this loyalty is presented with a light-ness of touch that allows us to accept it as part of the play's comic fantasy. But Frances, in *Ram Alley*, defends herself with a curious solemnity:

Believe me, love, howe'er some stricter wits
Condemn all women which are prone to love,

14 See Ernest Schanzer, 'The Marriage-Contracts in *Measure of Measure*,' *Shakespeare Survey* 13 (Cambridge, 1960), p. 83.

And think that if their favour fall on any,
By consequence they must be naught with many,
And hold a false position: that a woman,
False to herself, can trusty be to no man –
Yet no, I say: howe'er my life hath lost
The fame which my virginity aspir'd,
I will be true to thee: my deed shall move
To win from all men pity, if not love. (i.i.p.277)

This is one of the few moments of sentimentality in an otherwise brutally funny play. Barry has reversed one stereotype only to give us another – the tart with the heart of gold.

None of these attempts to complicate the conventional opposition of chaste maid and vicious whore really amounts to much: they are all minor effects, frequently uncertain and apologetic. The stereotype, in other words, seems difficult to break. But it *does* break, with a satisfying crash, in Middleton and Dekker's *The Roaring Girl* (Prince Henry's, *c.* 1610), where female chastity is embodied, not in a virtuous shopgirl, but in Moll Cutpurse, whose racy speech and intimate knowledge of the underworld might seem more appropriate to a conventional whore. The theatrical surface of one figure is superimposed on the moral values of the other, and the result establishes that virtue is not merely a matter of conventional images. This idea is asserted in various ways throughout the play, by other characters defending Moll – 'He hates unworthily, that by rote contemns, / For the name neither saves, nor yet condemns' (ii.ii.163–4) – and by Moll herself:

> 'cause you'll say
> I'm given to sport, I'm often merry, jest,
> Had mirth no kindred in the world but lust? (iii.i.99–101)

> How many are whores, in small ruffs, and still looks?
> How many chaste, whose names fill slander's books? (v.i.314–5)

Moll's language provides a deliberate reversal of the expected image of the chaste woman. She takes part in ribald conversations, as when she jokes with a tailor about putting a yard in her breeches (ii.ii.80–9), and even her assertions of chastity can be racy: 'all this while I was in a dream; one shall lie rudely then, but being awake, I keep my legs together' (iv.i.122–4). She is chaste, despite appearances; but her chastity is not obedience to a social or religious code: it is the assertion of an individual will. The independence that makes her scorn the usual images of respectability is also the key to her sexual behaviour. As she says when rejecting a proposal of marriage, 'I love to lie o' both sides o' th' bed myself' (II.ii.35–6).

We see this most clearly in the scene in which Laxton, a typical would-be seducer, finds that Moll is not so easy a target as he had assumed. She rebukes the gallant for his ill-founded vanity, and goes on to a broader denunciation of men of his type who assume that any woman will yield to them, and who destroy their reputations whether they do or not (III.i.68–80). [15] Moll declares herself above the snares of men, which trap more feeble-minded women, proudly rejects the name of whore and the censure of the world, and scorns the idea of submitting herself to any man. She then translates these assertions into action by fighting with Laxton and defeating him. In the soliloquy that follows, she takes the idea of independence a stage further. She refuses submission not only to men, but to her own physical nature:

> she that has wit, and spirit,
> May scorn to live beholding to her body for meat,
> Or for apparel like your common dame,
> That makes shame get her clothes, to cover shame.
> Base is that mind, that kneels unto her body,
> As if a husband stood in awe on's wife,
> My spirit shall be mistress of this house,
> As long as I have time in't. (III.i.133–40)

The idea of chastity is embodied in a colourful, individual personality, and even restraint and self-discipline become positive, not negative qualities. Like Simon Eyre, but in a more surprising way, she provides a thoroughly theatrical embodiment for a set of moral values. The play as a whole is a tired, conventional piece of work by two writers who had done the same thing before, and done it better; but Moll herself springs to life, and lingers in the memory. [16]

With the breaking of the theatrical stereotype comes a deeper exploration of one woman's reason for chastity. But such exploration is possible even in a play that keeps the usual dramatic surface unruffled. Like other dramatic

15 This is a standard charge against gallants, whose vanity is such that rather than appear as unsuccessful seducers they will slander women they have never lain with. See also *The Fair Maid of the Exchange*, ll.691–8, and Dekker and Webster's *Northward Ho*, i.i.

16 T.S. Eliot, *Elizabethan Dramatists* (London, 1963), pays just tribute to Moll as 'a real and unique human being' (p. 85), though his claim that she has 'renounced all happiness for herself' (p. 90) seems curious in view of the gusto with which she follows her chosen, eccentric way of life.

stereotypes (the citizen hero and citizen villain, for example) the figures of chaste maid and whore are logical enough to stand analysis by writers who are not content to present them in a routine manner. Nathan Field, in *Amends for Ladies* (Queen's Revels? c. 1611), presents the usual confrontation between a chaste woman and a cynical seducer, from the usual point of view, but he explores the rationale behind the convention in a way that takes the scene out of the ordinary. Bold, disguised as a waiting-woman, has contrived to get into bed with the widow Lady Bright; she discovers his true sex, and he asks her to yield herself to him. This she flatly refuses to do, saying that such a deed would confound her soul. The resulting debate relates the question of sexual morality to the very nature of man, and his place in the scheme of things. Bold argues that her soul cannot be harmed

> by such a natural act,
> Which beasts are born to and have privilege in.
> Fie, fie, if this could be, far happier
> Are sensitive souls in their creation
> Than man the prince of creatures; think you Heaven
> Regards such mortal deeds, or punisheth
> Those acts, for which He hath ordained us? (IV.i.88–94)

In her reply, she insists that God-given reason exalts man above the beasts, and the essence of his superiority is his ability to control his appetites; to yield to lust is not natural, but bestial:

> You argue like an atheist, man is never
> The prince of creatures, as you call him now,
> But in his reason, fail that, he is worse
> Than horse or dog, or beasts of wilderness;
> And 'tis that reason teacheth us to do
> Our actions unlike them; then, that which you
> Termed in them a privilege beyond us,
> The baseness of their being doth express,
> Compar'd to ours; horses, bulls, and swine
> Do leap their dams; because man does not so,
> Shall we conclude his making happiless? (IV.i.95–105)

Man has social and religious responsibilities which restrict the freedom of his animal nature, but which make him, at the same time, higher than the animals. An extra dimension is added to the scene by the fact that the lady loves Bold, and freely admits it. But her love, far from being a reason for yielding to him, is one of the must urgent reasons for remaining adamant against him: she does not want him to cheapen himself (IV.i.68–74). And, in fact, while he remains in the role of seducer, Bold cuts a shabby and even ridiculous figure. He is soundly beaten in the debate, and even his pride in the wit he has used to gain access to her is deflated:

BOLD
... newness of the trick,
If nothing else, might stir ye.
WIDOW
'Tis a stale one
And was done in the Fleet ten years ago;
Will you begone? The door is open for you. (IV.i.122–6)

The witty, successful seducer of Restoration comedy is rarely met with in these earlier plays. Bold is a more typical figure – a lecher who not only fails to justify himself intellectually, but finds that even his wit gets him nowhere. In the end, he gains the widow's bed, but only on orthodox moral terms, through marriage. Field here displays the usual absolute attitudes to chastity, but in deflating the seducer through both intellectual debate and comedy, he makes them more interesting than is often the case.

Field's examination of chastity shows that it is possible to do more than just set up the conventional figure and let her go through the motions. But his theatrical means are still fairly simple: the widow is put on display in the normal way, and simply allowed to talk more than usual. To see a greater variety of theatrical methods in examining the values behind a stereotype, we have to turn to two dramatizations of the figure of the whore, one by Dekker and one by Middleton. Dekker's two-part play The Honest Whore (Prince Henry's, 1604 and c. 1605), the first part written with Middleton, depends to a great extent on long, moralizing speeches to make its points; but other devices are employed, and I hope to show that they vary not just the dramatic mode of the play but the kind of insight it provides. Let us take the speeches first. In Part One Hippolito argues the whore Bellafront out of her trade, and in Part Two, having himself lapsed, he tries to argue her back into it, but she resists. Hippolito, in Part One, makes the usual points about the treachery of whoredom – 'A harlot is like Dunkirk, true to none' (II.i.353) – and its barren, destructive quality:

Why, those that love you, hate you ...
... and e'en curse
Their fruitless riot, for what one begets

Another poisons; lust and murder hit,
A tree being often shook, what fruit can knit? (II.i.346–51)

The act of love has been perverted into an act of destruction, of which the pox is the frightening symbol. As Bellafront herself says, after her conversion, ''stead of children, they breed rank diseases' (Part One, III.iii.57). She also plays on the connection between sexual and financial vice: 'that usury's worst of all, / When th'interest will eat out the principal' (Part One, III.iii.63–4).

These are standard arguments, though they are vividly expressed; but Dekker also makes the point, which is not so common, that a whore is her own worst enemy. Because she herself is untrustworthy, she can depend on no one, and form no solid attachments: 'Y'are like the Jews, scattered, in no place certain' (II.i.401). There has never been a whore, however successful she may have been at first, who did not end her life in poverty and disease: 'Diseases suck't her marrow, then grew so poor, / That she has begg'd, e'en at a beggar's door' (II.i.382–3). Her trade is essentially rootless and insecure, depending on momentary pleasures, with no solid basis for the future.

Bellafront herself points out that the whore is also victimized by men, who have to share the guilt for making her what she is. The unflattering picture of male lust in this play is, in itself, fairly typical; but to use this, as Dekker does, to make men share the guilt of prostitution is all too rare, and Dekker deserves considerable credit for it:

O siren's subtle tunes! Yourselves you flatter,
And our weak sex betray; so men love water,
It serves to wash their hands, but (being once foul)
The water down is poured, cast out of doors,
And even of such base use do men make whores. (Part Two, IV.i.317–21)

Prostitution is a cynical profession, but the cynicism is not all on one side. Bellafront's accusation is borne out by the conduct of Matheo, who, in Part One, is named as the man who first seduced her and made her a whore. Having ruined her, he refuses to make an honest woman of her by marriage. In Part Two, having been made to marry her, Matheo behaves just as badly, leading a life of debauchery and trying to persuade his wife to turn whore again in order to finance his riots. Nor does Hippolito himself make a much better showing in the second play. His attempt to seduce Bellafront consists of flimsy, specious, and cynical arguments, which she refutes with ease. This picture of whores as victims, both of their own trade, and of the cynicism of men, does not soften Dekker's criticism of the institution – quite the reverse, in fact – but it throws a more humane light on the role of the prostitute than do the rigid denunciations of conventional moralists.

Already we can see Dekker going beyond merely having his characters talk about prostitution: the responsibility of men is discussed by Bellafront, but it is also dramatized in the behaviour of Matheo and Hippolito. And there is a certain irony in the way the moralizing speeches operate in their dramatic context. Bellafront's repentance is not based entirely on moral argument. What Hippolito says strikes her deeply, because she is in love with him. One of the points he makes is that true love, as opposed to the love of a courtesan, demands exclusive loyalty: 'I must tell you Lady, were you mine, / You should be all mine; I could brook no sharers' (Part One, II.i.260–1). The realization that he cannot love her because of her whoredom is an important factor in her repentance, and perhaps the basic element in her new life is the abandonment of promiscuity and the devotion to one man. Her conversion to honesty is, however, gradual. She says that she has dreamed of being loyal to one man, but she thinks of this still in terms of her trade, and the dream includes some rather cynical fringe benefits:

Had I but met with one kind gentleman,
That would have purchas'd sin alone, to himself,
For his own private use, although scarce proper:
Indifferent handsome; meetly leg'd and thighed;
And my allowance reasonable – i'faith,
According to my body – by my troth,
I would have been as true unto his pleasures,
Yea, and as loyal to his afternoons,
As ever a poor gentlewoman could be. (Part One, II.i.268–76)

The principle of loyalty is there, and it will serve as the basis for her later honesty, but at this point it is still diluted with the self-interest of her trade: 'meetly leg'd and thighed; / And my allowance reasonable.' And indeed this self-interest is an important factor in her conversion, since Hippolito's sermon lays such stress on the disadvantages of prostitution from the whore's own point of view: 'Oh you have damnation without pleasure for it!' (II.i.419). By showing that Bellafront is not won over by the irresistible power of morality alone, Dekker makes the first stages of her repentance seem surprisingly honest and realistic. In particular, he shows that the prostitute's habits of thought are more deeply ingrained than the simple moral posturing would suggest. There is even a hint of duplicity, as well as of self-interest: 'poor gentlewoman' sounds suspiciously like a self-pitying euphemism.[17]

17 Normand Berlin, 'Thomas Dekker: a Partial Reappraisal,' SEL, VI (Spring 1966), 268, suggests, with some justice, that vanity also plays a part in Bellafront's conversion.

In Part Two, however, Bellafront becomes more a conventional 'chaste wife' figure. The self-interest has evaporated. She is married to Matheo, and loyal to him, despite his shabby treatment of her, and despite the fact that she is now, for the first time, offered the chance of Hippolito's love. Her reply to his attempt at seduction shows that her love for him has been transformed into the principle of loyalty to one man:

To prove a woman should not be a whore,
When she was made, she had one man, and no more,
Yet she was tied to laws then, for (even than)
'Tis said, she was not made for men, but man. (iv.i.301–4)

Her infatuation with Hippolito was the initial cause of her conversion, but she is capable of transcending it when virtue requires.

Some critics have regarded Bellafront as a major artistic success; Felix E. Schelling in particular is startlingly enthusiastic: 'There is no completer realization of human nature in the range of the drama than the character of Bellafronte in both her unreclaimed and in her repentant state.'[18] But for Una Ellis-Fermor she is 'a piece of sentimental and cheap idealism'[19] and one must admit that Dekker's dramatization of the whore's problems, though his ideas on the subject are more humane and intelligent than we often find, is marred by an overconscious striving for effect, particularly when we are called upon to admire her repentance. Bellafront herself is made to say

A woman honest first and then turn whore,
Is (as with me) common to thousands more,
But from a strumpet to turn chaste; that sound,
Has oft been heard, that woman hardly found. (Part One, iv.i.196–9)

She is saying, in effect, 'Look at me! See how virtuous I am!' and this sort of thing happens far too often in both plays. There are moments, especially just before her repentance, when Bellafront is convincing, but in the long run she is nothing more nor less than a successful figure of melodrama. She is a vehicle for some lively rhetoric, and some effective dramatic poses, but the stuff of life is not in her.

The fact that Dekker's imagination is not as deeply engaged in the creation of Bellafront as it might be is indicated by the way he occasionally allows the

18 *Elizabethan Drama 1558–1642* (New York, 1959), 1,338–9
19 *The Jacobean Drama* (London, 1958), p. 125

conventional jokes about prostitution to undermine her moralizing. When she denounces the pander Roger, his unabashed reply is rather amusing:

BELLAFRONT

...

Thou, that slave to sixpence, base-mettl'd villain.

ROGER

Sixpence? Nay, that's not so; I never took under two shillings fourpence, I hope I know my fee. (Part One, iii.ii.48–50)

Roger's reply, if analysed, shows how feeble his own moral responses are, but the immediate dramatic effect is that he has scored a point, and deflated Bellafront's solemn moralizing. Dekker seems, at this point, to be more interested in making an effect, any effect, than in preserving the moral integrity of his play.

More convincing than the moralizing of Bellafront is the Bridewell scene at the end of Part Two, in which unrepentant whores are portrayed with brutal realism. Dorothea Target, the first to be brought forward, scorns the thought of repentant tears: 'Say ye? Weep? Yes forsooth, as you did when you lost your maidenhead; do you not hear how I weep? (Sings)' (v.ii.297–8). Another, Penelope Whorehound, makes a great display of lamentation and begging for bail – but we learn that this is an act she puts on regularly, and that she is in reality a hardened reprobate. These unsentimental portrayals have a documentary quality; Dekker here displays a tough frankness that makes the repentant whore seem by comparison a wraith, a pale figure created by sentimentality. The play's lectures on prostitution seem academic by comparison with this dramatization of the real thing. In the last analysis, then, the achievement of *The Honest Whore* is uneven, and its vision is disjointed; but in its best scenes Dekker expands his dramatic range well beyond the conventional stage sermons, even if those sermons contain some unusually shrewd insights.

Middleton, in *Michaelmas Term* (Paul's, c. 1606), also analyses what prostitution does to those who practise it, and his analysis, though less detailed than Dekker's, is more fully dramatic. His medium is ironic rather than moralistic comedy, and his emphasis is accordingly on the deceptiveness, the false values of the trade: the usual jokes are given a keener cutting edge. Prostitution is made part of the interplay of town and country on which the comedy is based. The Country Wench, tempted by the glamour of London, has come there to lead a life of sin.[20] Her motive is not simply sensuality, but the same desire

20 Ruby Chatterji has pointed out that the fall of the Country Wench parallels the fall of Easy in the main plot. See 'Unity and Disparity in *Michaelmas Term*,' *SEL*, viii (Spring 1968), 350–1.

for social prestige that inspires the play's other social climbers, Quomodo and Andrew Lethe. Talking with the pander Hellgill, she tries to claim that she would otherwise have been chaste: 'If I had not a desire to go like a gentlewoman, you should be hang'd ere you should get me to't, I warrant you' (I.ii.27–8). Hellgill's reply is cynical but telling: 'I know you are all chaste enough, / Till one thing or another tempt you!' (I.ii.31–2). Her values are distorted, so that finery matters more than chastity, and she tries to pass off her sin as excusable on those grounds. Her fine city clothes go to her head, so that she tries to deny her lowly country origins; in a sense, she is taken in by her own disguise:

HELLGILL
Who would think now this fine sophisticated squall came out of the bosom of a barn, and the loins of a hay-tosser?
WENCH
Out, you saucy, pestiferous pander! I scorn that, i'faith.
HELLGILL
Excellent, already the true phrase and style of a strumpet. (III.i.22–5)

The false values of her trade are such that she denies even her own identity. When Hellgill comments that her own father would not know her, she replies, 'How can he know me, when I scarce know myself?' (III.i.30–1). This turns out to be literally true. Her father comes to town in disguise to look for her; he joins her service, thinking at first that she is a fine lady, and even when he realizes the truth and denounces her as a strumpet, he does not know it is his own daughter he is rebuking. In comedy, mistakes of identity are normally sorted out, but in this case the play ends with father and daughter still unknown to each other. This is a parallel to the case of Andrew Lethe, formerly Andrew Gruel, who has even changed his name to satisfy his social pretensions, and whose own mother serves him without knowing who he is. In the end, Lethe and the Country Wench are made to marry each other, and it seems a comic punishment for their having sinned in the same way. Disguises and mistaken identity, which so often are only plot devices, take on symbolic force here, showing how the pretensions which are part of the courtesan's trade can destroy her very identity.

This point is made implicitly, through the action. While there is also some verbal criticism of the courtesan, the best of this is also implicit, conveyed through the imagery. At one point Hellgill offers an amusing, ironic defence of whoredom:

Why, therefore take heart, faint not at all,
Women ne'er rise but when they fall;

Let a man break, he's gone, blown up,
A woman's breaking sets her up;
Virginity is no city trade,
You're out o'th'freedom, when you're a maid;
Down with the lattice, 'tis but thin,
Let coarser beauties work within,
Whom the light mocks; thou art fair and fresh,
The gilded flies will light upon thy flesh. (I.ii.39–48)

It all seems quite cheerful, until the sudden sting of the last line, in which the image of fly-blown flesh reveals the corruption beneath the glamour of prostitution, and casts an ironic light on the rest of the speech. The flies are 'gilded,' just as the glory Hellgill offers is gilded, not pure gold, and hides corruption. The most effective comment from the wench's father, who acts as a moral chorus throughout the play, comes when he picks up this image: 'But I scarce like my mistress now; the loins / Can ne'er be safe where the flies be so busy' (III.i.108–9).

His more explicit moralizing sermons, of which there are many, are less effective. Sermons are not Middleton's strong point, though he occasionally turns a neat phrase, as when the father offers the standard black-and-white view of the fallen woman: 'One minute, and eternally undone' (II.ii.30). For the most part, the father goes on in this vein:

Thou fair and wicked creature, steep'd in art,
Beauteous and fresh, the soul the foulest part!
A common filth is like a house possess'd,
Where, if not spoil'd, you'll come out fray'd at least.
This service likes not me; though I rest poor,
I hate the basest use, to screen a whore.
The human stroke n'er made him; he that can
Be bawd to woman never leapt from man;
Some monster won his mother. (III.i.259–67)

The ideas are stated abstractly, and connected with the imagery rather than expressed through it. Consequently, both the images and the ideas have a weakened impact. As in the Quomodo plot of the same play, the most effective criticism is not the explicit, external judgments of sermons and court sentences, but the implicit commentary made by the action itself. And the verbal judgments are most effective when they are not stated abstractly, but realized in imagery.

The comic indulgence which modifies the judgments of the Quomodo plot is present here as well, though much less prominent. The whore is allowed, at one point, a comic defence of her trade which, though it certainly cannot be accepted at its face value, has a cheerful flippancy that disarms criticism: 'Do not all trades live by their ware, and yet call'd honest livers? Do they not thrive best when they utter most, and make it away by the great? Is not wholesale the chiefest merchandise? Do you think some merchants could keep their wives so brave, but for their wholesale? You're foully deceiv'd and you think so' (IV.ii.10–16). She is not the only one who uses sex for money; her trade is simply the way of the world. But this comic indulgence is only a momentary effect, and it is offset by a serious weight of criticism elsewhere. For the most part, the comedy surrounding the country wench is used to comment on the false values of her trade, and the judgment passed is firm and effective.

However, joking about prostitution cannot always be so easily accommodated with a moral analysis of it. One play which extends its range in this way, and extends it to the point of breakdown, is Edward Sharpham's *The Fleer* (Queen's Revels, 1606). Fleer, the title character, acts as a servant to the two whores Florida and Felicia. He offers, at one point, a conventional comic defence of their trade, seeing it as an honest commercial enterprise: 'They forswear not themselves, in commendation of their wares, as your common tradesmen do, swearing they cannot afford it at the price. They are no proverb breakers, beware the buyer say they, you shall have enough for your money, if half will not serve your turn take the whole, measure with your own yard, you shall have Winchester measure.' (sig. C⁴r). ('Winchester measure' is standard measure, but the area surrounding Winchester house was notorious for brothels, and the expression therefore has other connotations. There are also the usual puns on 'whole' and 'yard.') The cheerful, flippant tone indicates an acceptance of the trade; if there is irony, it is too light to have much critical effect. And Fleer throws himself into the business of pandering with unabashed gusto: 'Come, come, I'll put you in the way of all flesh, I'll send you to Gravesend, I'll see you in the tilt-boat; when you are there, ship yourselves: in, in, in … I have shipp'd two gallants in a storm, I fear they have spent their mainmasts by this time, and are coming home again; but if you will southwards, my hearts of gold, I'll ship you in pomp, I'll send ye under the very line, where the sun's at hottest' (sig.E¹r). The joking conveys a sense of gleeful participation, of the sort that we find in *Ram Alley*. What makes it startling is that Fleer is really the courtesans' father, serving them in disguise, and supposedly acting as a moral agent to reclaim them from whoredom. Sharpham uses the basic *How a Man May Choose* plot to illustrate the murderous treachery of whores, and the play contains moralizing comments from Fleer himself about the folly and evil of their trade (sigs.C³v-⁴r). But the real energy of the play lies in the bawdy jokes, which turn the occasional statements of moral intention into empty poses and the murder plot into lightweight melodrama with no serious moral pressure behind it. When Fleer says, 'Heaven I know has grace enough in store, / To make most chaste, a most lascivious whore' (sig.E²r), we find it hard to believe that he means it, in view of the obvious delight he takes in pandering.

There is, however, one play that does extend its range to include both joking and sermonizing, and a good deal more, without falling to pieces in the process – John Marston's *The Dutch Courtesan* (Queen's Revels, c. 1604). Here several of the attitudes we have noticed in other plays – notably confident sermons against unchastity, and joking acceptance of it – are examined critically as part of a careful exploration of the whole problem. It is Malheureux who, in the play's early scenes, speaks with the accents of conventional morality, seeing sexual questions as matters of absolute good and evil: 'Know, sir, the strongest argument that speaks / Against the soul's eternity is lust' (i.i.81–2). The glib, aphoristic quality in his speech puts us on guard; he is altogether too sure of himself. Freevill, his more easy-going friend, pokes fun at his tendency to reduce sexual problems to moral epigrams; he has been persuading Malheureux to come with him to the courtesan Franceschina, and Malheureux finally agrees:

MALHEUREUX
Well, I'll go to make her loathe the shame she's in.
The sight of vice augments the hate of sin.
FREEVILL
The sight of vice augments the hate of sin!
Very fine, perdy! (i.i.152–5)

Unfortunately for Malheureux, the sight of vice does no such thing. Thinking in absolutes, he assumes (as conventional moralists do) that vice will have a repulsive appearance to match its inner nature; he is baffled and disturbed to find that Franceschina is beautiful: 'Are strumpets, then, such things so delicate? / Can custom spoil what nature made so good?' (i.ii.129–30). He has been going on theory, not experience, and when he meets an actual whore his theory lets him down. He becomes infatuated with her, and his lust, when awakened, is all the stronger for having been repressed. As Crispinella, sister of Freevill's fiancée Beatrice, remarks 'as in the fashion of time, those books that are call'd in are most in sale and request, so in nature those actions that are most prohibited are most desired' (iii.i.41–4).

Merely to preach against lust, then, is an inadequate response to it. The other possibility is joking acceptance, and there are those who have felt that this attitude is so powerful in *The Dutch Courtesan* that it sabotages the play's morality.[21] It is certainly present, but whether it has quite this effect is another question. Freevill and the 'witty city jester' Cocledemoy provide conventional joking defences of prostitution, in which the evils and dangers are either glossed over or presented, with cynical irony, as virtues. Freevill comments, in debate with Malheureux, 'I would have married men love the stews as Englishmen lov'd the Low Countries: wish war should be maintain'd there lest it should come home to their own doors' (1.i.62–5). Cocledemoy makes the conventional link with commerce:

Her shop has the best ware; for where these [i.e., tradesmen] sell but cloth, satins, and jewels, she sells divine virtues as virginity, modesty, and such rare gems, and those not like a petty chapman, by retail, but like a great merchant, by wholesale. ... Again, whereas no trade or vocation profiteth but by the loss and displeasure of another – as the merchant thrives not but by the licentiousness of giddy and unsettled youth, the lawyer but by the vexation of his client, the physician but by the maladies of his patient – only my smooth-gumm'd bawd lives by others' pleasure, and only grows rich by others' rising. O merciful gain! O righteous income! (1.ii.35–48)

There is a bit of truth in these joking defences: brothels do provide pleasure instead of preying on misfortune, and perhaps reduce the amount of adultery by directing the energies of lecherous young men another way. But the main impression here is of cynical, sophistic half-truths, and of vices twisted into virtues for the sake of amusement.

I think, however, that these speeches can be distinguished from the speeches, let us say, of Fleer, in which the jokes destroy the moral basis of the play. Fleer is in a position to act as a moral commentator, and does so only fitfully. Cocledemoy, on the other hand, is simply a wag; because he jokes about whoredom, this does not mean that the play as a whole treats the subject lightly. Freevill, though he does act as a moral spokesman elsewhere, is speaking now before the full viciousness of the whore has been revealed to him; he can still regard whoredom as to some extent a laughing matter. Also, we should consider the dramatic situation: Freevill is in conversation with his austere friend, whose extreme views he finds foolish. It is reasonable to suggest that he is teasing Malheureux, deliberately saying things that will shock him. Marston, in these

---

21 See, for example, Esther Cloudman Dunn, *Ben Jonson's Art: Elizabethan Life and Literature as Reflected Therein* (Northampton, Mass., 1925), pp. 131–2; and John Peter, 'John Marston's Plays,' *Scrutiny*, XVII (Summer 1950), 152–3.

speeches, is representing one view of whoredom – joking, cynical acceptance. But he has left open the possibility that the final statement of the play may be something quite different.

Freevill himself outgrows this attitude fairly soon. His impure love for the courtesan is driven out by his honest love for Beatrice, and when he sees the completely different way the two women behave, his flippancy drops from him altogether:

> What man, but worthy name of man, would leave
> The modest pleasures of a lawful bed,
> The holy union of two equal hearts,
> ...
> To twine th'unhealthful loins of common loves,
> The prostituted impudence of things
> Senseless like those by cataracts of Nile,
> Their use so vile takes away sense! How vile
> To love a creature made of blood and hell,
> Whose use makes weak, whose company doth shame,
> Whose bed doth beggar, issue doth defame! (v.i.67–9, 73–9)

His early jesting was as glib and thoughtless as the moralizing of Malheureux, and he has outgrown it. His ideas on whoredom are now rather like those of Malheureux at the beginning, but they are more solid because they are based on knowledge, not theory.

Malheureux progresses to a similar revulsion based on knowledge; in a sense, he discovers that he was right in the first place, but the important point is that he now knows *why* he was right. Franceschina is stung to the quick by Freevill's desertion of her, and her price for sleeping with Malheureux is that he should kill Freevill. When he tells her that he has done so, instead of keeping her promise she has him arrested; this is the murderous treachery of the whore, as shown in such plays as *How a Man May Choose a Good Wife from a Bad*. But while in that play the whore's revelation of her true nature destroys the hero's infatuation at once, Marston sees that human behaviour is not that simple. Malheureux's conversion is slow, difficult, and painful – much more so than Freevill's. His infatuation has so weakened his moral nature that he envies the 'happy beasts, / In whom an inborn heat is not held sin' (ii.i.72–3). Not only that but he is genuinely (though briefly) tempted by the idea of killing his friend to win the whore: 'The body of a man is of the selfsame soil / As ox or horse; no murder to kill those' (ii.ii.201–2). While it was necessary for him to acknowledge his animal nature, he has gone too far, and actually surrendered to it. And even when he has rejected the idea of murder, his lust is such that he still desires Franceschina's body though he knows the foulness of her soul. To cure him of this, Freevill has to take drastic measures. He offers to go into hiding so that Malheureux can pretend he has killed him and claim his reward from the whore. Franceschina then betrays Malheureux, and since Freevill is nowhere to be found, no one believes the story that he has gone into hiding, and the supposed murderer is brought to the gallows. He repents, finally and fully, with the rope around his neck. Only when the murderous treachery of the whore has been directed against him does he completely reject her. It is a sad comment on the damage done to his moral sense that such extreme measures have to be used.

As Freevill himself admits, this plot has a streak of evil in it: it is terribly cruel. But man is such a flawed creature that he cannot be reclaimed by morality alone. When Freevill urges his friend to call reason and religion to quench his desire, Malheureux replies 'There is no God in blood, no reason in desire' (iv.ii.13). His animal side, once roused, must be appealed to on its own terms – in this case, force and self-interest. Freevill, commenting on his own plot, realizes this:

But is this virtue in me? No, not pure;
Nothing extremely best with us endures.
No use in simple purities; the elements
Are mix'd for use. Silver without alloy
Is all too eager to be wrought for use:
Nor precise virtues ever purely good
Holds useful size with temper of weak blood. (iv.ii.39–45)

It is worth noting, in connection with this speech, that even Freevill's use of disappearance and disguise to teach himself to appreciate his wife's virtues has its evil side. He savours her display of grief too smugly, and in so doing delays too long in telling her he is alive; in the end, he realizes this, and begs forgiveness. In this play, even the moral agent who tests and corrects the other characters is examined and found wanting.

Marston shows a world in which moral problems are too complex to be solved easily,[22] but the problems are at least clearly stated. There is at the heart of

---

22 G.K. Hunter observes a 'sense of restriction in the victory' at the end of the play; see 'English Folly and Italian Vice: The Moral Landscape of John Marston,' *Stratford-upon-Avon Studies I: Jacobean Theatre*, ed. John Russell Brown and Bernard Harris (London, 1960), p. 111. I would rather say that the victory is achieved at considerable cost, and by means that are not always attractive.

the play a firm idea of right and wrong in sexual relationships. Personal loyalty, a theme we have noticed in other plays, is what sanctifies sex. The devotion of Freevill to Beatrice, Beatrice's intense loyalty to her husband, and the hearty mutual regard of Crispinella and Tysefew – these are relationships based on personal affection, in which sensuality is perfectly proper.[23] The improper relationships – Freevill's casual indulgences with Franceschina, Franceschina's possessive, destructive, essentially selfish passion for Freevill, Malheureux's desire for the courtesan's body in spite of his abhorrence for the woman herself – these are relationships without loyalty. Here, there is no sanction for sensuality, and it becomes purely lust. In the end, Marston leaves the traditional opposition of chaste maid and vicious whore undisturbed.

While the underlying moral code is orthodox, the play's real power lies in its admission that the code is cruelly difficult to obey, that the choices it demands are not easy to make, and that sometimes only sin itself can drive out sin. This is potentially a tragic vision, though it is kept comic by the happy ending that rescues Malheureux from the full consequences of his passion, and by the rhetorical exaggeration of Marston's style, which emphasizes the absurdity rather than the enormity of his characters' excesses. It would be possible, by quoting speeches out of context, to 'demonstrate' that this play is conventionally moral, or conventionally flippant, on the question of sexual morality. But the conventional, discursive passages one would quote in the course of such an argument are, in fact, carefully and often ironically placed in the context of speaker and situation. The confident poses struck by the characters, whether they are preaching against lust or trying to excuse it, are laughably empty when set against the reality of their own complex, intractable natures. Marston, in this play at least, goes beyond conventional responses to a careful analysis of 'that subtle knot, which makes us man.'

23 See Paul M. Zall, 'John Marston, Moralist,' *ELH*, xx (September 1953), 193.

7
The comedy of intrigue: adultery

BIANCA
To bed, to bed.
MALEVOLE
Do your husbands lie with you?
BIANCA
That were country-fashion, i'faith.
Marston, *The Malcontent*

Several of the motifs I have traced in previous chapters come together in comedies dealing with adultery. The basic, conventional attitudes to sexual morality – absolute insistence on a stern moral code, and joking acceptance of vice – are combined with a concern for the special problems of marriage, the responsibility that husband and wife have to each other. In some cases the combination of attitudes is quite intricate; but there are many simple, conventional plays, which take a single attitude and stick to it, and I should like to take a brief look at some of these before going on to consider more complex works.

In the moral comedies of the public theatres, there is the usual celebration of female chastity, as opposed to the lechery and cynicism of men.[1] We see the familiar figure of the chaste woman fending off incompetent seducers; but this

---

1 This pro-feminism is continued and expanded in Caroline drama. Clifford Leech, *Shakespeare's Tragedies and Other Studies in Seventeenth Century Drama* (London, 1950), pp. 170–1, suggests that Caroline dramatists were particularly conscious of the influence of women in the audience. Pro-feminism in Caroline drama is discussed in detail by Douglas Sedge, 'Social and Ethical Concerns in Caroline Drama,' unpublished PH D dissertation (University of Birmingham, 1966), pp. 137–89.

time her responsibility is not merely to her own chastity but to her husband's honour as well.[2] Since her husband is often one of the enemies of her chastity, her testing is more elaborate than that of the chaste maid figure. The prodigal husband, who bullies and ill-treats his wife, is used to throw her patience, loyalty, and chastity into high relief in such conventional moral plays as *How a Man May Choose a Good Wife from a Bad* (Worcester's, c. 1602) and *The Fair Maid of Bristow* (King's, c. 1604). The jealous husband is a variation on this type, and is conventionally set against the figure of the chaste wife. Vaster, in *The Honest Lawyer*, by 'S.S.' (Queen Anne's, c. 1615), out of a mistaken contempt for his wife's honesty, sells her as a prostitute. Sir Timothy Troublesome, in Edward Sharpham's *Cupid's Whirligig* (King's Revels, 1607), gelds himself on the grounds that if his wife then becomes pregnant, his suspicions will be confirmed. One excess is melodramatic, the other farcical; both emphasize that the husband is the real threat to the marriage, while the wife's virtue, tested and proved, is what saves it in the end.[3] (In fact, Vaster's wife, like Marina in *Pericles*, annoys her employer by preaching morality to all the customers who come to the brothel.)

A more direct threat is the pandering husband – like Matheo in Dekker's *The Honest Whore, Part Two* (Prince Henry's, c. 1605), who urges his wife Bellafront to return to her old trade in order to finance his prodigality. One of the livelier treatments of this situation is found in Middleton's *Anything for a Quiet Life*, possibly written with Webster (King's, c. 1621). Knavesby, a scoundrel who is eager for wealth and preferment, wants to prostitute his wife to Lord Beaufort for the sake of his own advancement. Unlike the wronged but patient wives of more conventional plays, she defends herself with wit and spirit by making both men face the consequences of their desires. She pretends to Lord Beaufort that she has become infatuated with his page, and he is furious:

2　The special importance of a wife's chastity is indicated by Robert Cleaver, *A godlie forme of hovsehold government* ... (London, 1598): 'there is no honour within the house, longer than a man's wife is honourable' (p. 171). The point is expanded by Thomas Heywood in *Gunaikeion* (London, 1624): 'For virtue once violated, brings infamy and dishonour, not only to the person offending, but contaminates the whole progeny; nay more, looks back even to the injured ashes of the ancestors, be they never so noble: for the mind, as the body, in the act of adultery being both corrupted, makes the action infamous and dishonourable, dispersing the poison of the sin even amongst those from whom she derives her birth; as if with her earthly being they had given her therewith her corruptions, and the first occasion of this her infamy' (p. 164).

3　The destructiveness of jealousy becomes actually murderous in Robert Armin's *Two Maids of More-clacke* (King's Revels, c. 1608), in which Sir William plans to poison his 'wife' for cuckolding him. In fact, the woman he regards as his wife is not legally married to him, and the man she has been sleeping with is her real husband.

BEAUFORT
Sure you are a common creature.
MRS. KNAVESBY
                    Did you doubt it?
Wherefore came I hither else? Did you think
That honesty only had been immur'd for you,
And I should bring it as an offertory
Unto your shrine of lust? (III.i.131–6)

And she flings Knavesby's snobbery back at him by pretending that she has given herself to Lord Beaufort, and scorning her husband as beneath the notice of a nobleman's whore:

Never touch me more ...
I have kiss'd Ambition, and I love it,
I loathe the memory of every touch
My lip hath tasted from thee.
...
For thy pander's fee,
It shall be laid under the candlestick;
Look for't, I'll leave it for thee. (IV.ii.16–22, 38–40)

The effect is somewhat marred by a swift, perfunctory reconciliation in the last scene – the tensions between the characters are too great to be resolved so easily – but in the early scenes Mistress Knavesby is allowed a lively counterattack against her male aggressors.

The jealous husband and the pandering husband are both, essentially, acting out of contempt for their wives; and the two figures are actually fused in Sir John Loveall in Field's *Amends for Ladies* (Queen's Revels? c. 1611), who sets out to prove his suspicions by urging his friend Subtle to tempt his wife. At first, his motive seems to be simply to see how she will act, and to strengthen her chastity if she is in fact chaste (I.i.463–6). But he is, in reality, deeply cynical about women (III.i.4–11), and he would rather have his jealous fantasy come true than be proved wrong:

SUBTLE
Why tell me truly, would it please you best,
To have her remain chaste, or conquered?

SIR JOHN
Oh friend, 'twould do me good e'en at the heart
To have her overcome, she does so brag
And stand upon her chastity forsooth. (v.i.7–11)

He himself is paying court (unsuccessfully) to another woman; and he seems to be in the grip of an instinctive urge to drag his wife down to his own level. But the lady holds out, and, in a final tableau, both men kneel to her, acknowledge her chastity, and beg forgiveness.

Perhaps this persistent denigration of male pomposity, cynicism, and lechery, as compared with female chastity, is a reaction against the domination of the husband in marriage, as well as a plea against the old-fashioned view that women are weak by nature and ready to fall at the first temptation.[4] Certainly it brings together a number of conventions whose popularity we have seen elsewhere: the insistence on marriage as a gently balanced partnership, the celebration of female chastity,[5] the critical treatment of prodigal and philandering men. But another conventional attitude we have seen is a casual, joking acceptance of sex. And curiously, the same pattern of sympathies can be seen in those bawdier comedies where the wife *does* fall when pushed as we see in the moral comedies where she stands fast. When a wife is matched with a bad husband, her chastity (in one kind of play) is admirable, and her unchastity (in the other kind) is excusable. In particular, her adultery can be a satisfying comic revenge against a bad husband. Antonio, the title character of Beaumont and Fletcher's *The Coxcomb* (Queen's Revels, *c.* 1609), is so eager to be famous for his friendship with Mercury that he offers him his wife Maria. Mercury feels a few temporary scruples, but Maria – acting from exasperation as much as anything – decides to take the opportunity, playing in an ironic way the role of the obedient wife: 'He is my husband, and 'tis reasonable he should command in

4 See Hardin Craig, *The Enchanted Glass* (Oxford, 1952), p. 131.
5 As we saw in chapter 6, the figure of the chaste woman – wife or maid – is usually just presented to us, and the roots of her behaviour are not examined. An interesting exception is *Grim the Collier of Croydon* (Admiral's? 1604), possibly by William Haughton. Honorea is trapped into a wealthy, loveless match with the old Earl of Kent; she attempts an affair with her lover Musgrave (whom she had wanted to marry), but their appointment is kept instead by a devil disguised as Musgrave, who lectures her on the value of chastity, and converts her. (One of the interesting features of this play is that the devils act as spokesmen and agents for conventional morality; even the synod of Hell, which opens and closes the play, is like a League of Decency meeting, with the devils deploring the goings-on upstairs.) But while the conversion of a romantic young girl into a chaste matron reverses the conventional comic sympathy for romantic love, the element of trickery in the conversion makes it, finally, less serious and interesting than it might have been.

all things; since he will be an ass against the hair, at his own peril be it' (IV.vi.26–8). Her adultery is simply a good joke against her idiotic husband. In Marston's *Jack Drum's Entertainment* (Paul's, *c.* 1600), Brabant Senior, who fancies himself as a wit and a practical joker, plans to gull the comic Frenchman John fo de King by presenting Mistress Brabant to him as a courtesan, confidently expecting that she will send the Frenchman packing. The latter is a clumsy buffoon, whose earlier attempts to get a wench have ended in humiliation; but Mistress Brabant submits at once to his broken-English wooing, and the joke recoils on her husband. The whole affair is treated as a jest, and the cuckold takes his punishment in a sporting manner: 'Wear the horn? Aye, spite of all your teeth, / I'll wear the crown, and triumph in this horn' (v.i.p. 240).[6]

In other cases, the joking springs not from the comic chastisement of the husband in particular, but from farcical situations in which any one of the parties is liable to be caught out – and sometimes all of them are. In William Percy's *The Cuck-queans and Cuckolds Errants* (privately acted? 1601) two husbands seduce each other's wives (each lecturing his own wife on the evils of adultery), and the situation provides some enjoyable, if obvious, irony at the expense of all parties. In the subplot to Robert Davenport's *A New Trick to Cheat the Devil* (Queen Henrietta's? *c.* 1625) a friar plays a practical joke on an adulterous innkeeper's wife and her lover, the village constable. The incident is in the fabliau tradition of practical jokes based on adultery.[7]

This rapid survey shows something of the possible range of treatments of adultery in citizen comedy, from moral assertion of chastity to bawdy joking. Most of the plays mentioned are content to select one kind of treatment, and keep to it, with simple and conventional – though sometimes entertaining – results. But one feels a deeper interest in those more ambitious plays which, like *The Dutch Courtesan*, try to combine more than one attitude into a larger dramatic whole, even if they run the risk of falling apart in the process. The risk is particularly great in comedies of intrigue which combine moral and social commentary with the amoral fun of trickery. I would now like to look at a number of more elaborate comedies of adultery, in which a fully developed intrigue is combined with some attempt at commentary, and to examine the opportunities, the tensions, and the compromises resulting from this combination. This will also provide an opportunity for a last look at three of the most

---

6 Worth mentioning here is the Cambridge comedy *Club Law* (Clare Hall, *c.* 1599), where the lustfulness of the citizens' wives is part of the play's depiction of the local town-and-gown war, and is just one more joke to fire at the local burghers.

7 For the fabliau which provided Davenport's source, see Charles Read Baskervill, *The Elizabethan Jig* (Chicago, 1929), pp. 326–30.

active and interesting writers of citizen comedy – Dekker, Middleton, and Jonson – and finally for a glance at Shakespeare's only contribution to the genre.

The two main plots of Dekker and Webster's *Westward Ho* (Paul's, 1604) appear at first glance to present radically different treatments of adultery. The plots are linked by the Italian merchant Justiniano, who, furious at his wife's supposed infidelity, determines to unmask the immorality of all city wives. While one plot shows his wife defending her chastity, the other shows Justiniano, disguised as a writing-master, providing the wives of three London merchants with gallants and arranging secret meetings for them. The wives at first respond with an eagerness that confirms his low estimation of their morals, and the tone of these early scenes is one of joking acceptance of immorality: as Justiniano says, when tempting one of his pupils, 'therefore sweet scholar, sugared Mistress Honeysuckle, take summer before you, and lay hold of it! Why, even now must you and I hatch an egg of iniquity' (ii.i.192–4). The women agree to go to 'Brainford' (the modern Brentford) with their gallants and spend the night there; the audience assumes, as the gallants do, that the affair will be consummated, but we are all in for a surprise. The wives are willing to flirt with the men, but no more; and their sense of mischief, which led them to Brainford, leads them to lock the doors when they get there:[8] 'They shall know that citizens' wives have wit enough to outstrip twenty such gulls; though we are merry, let's not be mad; be as wanton as new married wives, as fantastic and light-headed to the eye, as feather-makers, but as pure about the heart, as if we dwelt amongst 'em in Blackfriars' (v.i.159–63). Their peculiar view of chastity might not please a strict moralist,[9] but the authors seem to feel that the women can play with fire and not be burned.

Their delight in frustrating their lovers is accompanied by a genuine – if somewhat casual and condescending – affection for their husbands: 'Our honest husbands, they (silly men) lie praying in their beds now, that the water under

---

8 A curious feature in the criticism of the play is the number of times this development in the fifth act has been ignored. For example, Esther Cloudman Dunn, *Ben Jonson's Art: Elizabethan Life and Literature as Reflected Therein* (Northampton, Mass., 1925), writes that the comedy is 'made out of the careless insolence of gallants and the awed submission of citizens' wives to their advances' (p. 128). See also Brian Gibbons, *Jacobean City Comedy* (London, 1968), p. 137. In this play, and its sequel *Northward Ho*, middle-class characters are seen having the last laugh on gallants; yet both plays are persistently – and I think mistakenly – quoted as examples of the anti-citizen bias of the private theatres. See, for example, Louis B. Wright, *Middle-Class Culture in Elizabethan England* (Chapel Hill, 1935), p. 630.

9 Cf. Richard Brathwait, *The English Gentlewoman* (London, 1631): 'It is dangerous to enter parley with a beleaguering enemy; it implies want or weakness in the besieged. Chastity is like an enclosed garden, it should not be so much as assaulted, lest the report of her spotless beauty become soiled' (p. 42).

us may not be rough, the tilt that covers us may not be rent, and the straw about our feet may keep our pretty legs warm. I warrant they walk upon Queen-hive (as Leander did for Hero) to watch for our landing, and should we wrong such kind hearts? Would we might ever be troubled with the toothache then' (v.iv.118–24). But their 'honest husbands,' far from waiting meekly at home, are on their way to Brainford, led by Justiniano, and hot with indignation. When they arrive, however, the tables are turned on them as they were on the gallants. Not only are their suspicions proved groundless, but their own clandestine visits to the establishment of the bawd Birdlime are revealed. Male lechery is once again exposed and mocked, but with no particular moral severity: the reaction of the wives is one part indignation and three parts wry amusement: 'Have we smelt you out, foxes? ... Do you come after us with hue and cry when you are the thieves yourselves?' (v.iv.236–8). Female chastity is preserved, male lechery is mocked – but it is all done in a casual, joking manner.[10]

The tone of the other plot, in which a lecherous old Earl tries to seduce Mistress Justiniano, seems at first glance more earnest. She has been abandoned by her husband and is afraid that she may be forced to accept the Earl's proposition in order to survive; but her attitude to vice is merely a reluctant acceptance of it as better than starvation (I.i.203–5). When she sees the Earl, however, she is revolted by the picture of aged lechery he presents – 'I wonder lust can hang at such white hairs' (II.ii.83) – and rejects him indignantly. In their second meeting, the connection between lust and physical ugliness is made more explicit, and the seriousness of the earlier scene becomes melodrama. The Earl thinks he is about to entertain Mistress Justiniano; but it is really her husband, disguised as a woman and masked, who arrives. When the Earl takes off the mask he finds, as he thinks, a hideous old woman. Justiniano insists that he is the same woman the Earl courted before; the association of lust and ugliness reminds us of the shock his wife received in the earlier scene. He then announces that he poisoned his wife rather than have her submit to shame, and shows the Earl the body. She is not really dead, of course, but even when this fact is revealed, the knowledge that she would have killed herself rather than submit to the Earl is enought to convert him:

JUSTINIANO
Do not these open cuts now, cool your back?

10 The central device of surprise – the citizens' wives who appear casual about virtue, but who turn out to be chaste – seems to have been popular, for Dekker and Middleton tried to elaborate on it in the sub-plot of *The Roaring Girl* (Prince Henry's, *c.* 1610). Here, however, the characters' changes of attitude are so frequent, arbitrary, and finally confused, that it is difficult to make out what the authors' purposes are, and even more difficult to care.

Methinks they should; when Vice sees with broad eyes
Her ugly form, she does herself despise.

EARL
Mirror of dames, I look upon thee now,
As men long blind, having recovered sight,
Amaz'd; scarce able to endure the light;
Mine own shame strikes me dumb; henceforth the book
I'll read shall be thy mind, and not thy look. (IV.ii.159–66)

The stress on sight and appearance in these speeches is, I think, connected with the two revelations of physical ugliness that symbolize the moral ugliness of lust. It is not, perhaps, a very profound form of moral judgment – we remember Marston's attack on it in *The Dutch Courtesan* – but it has a certain theatrical effectiveness.

The writing in these scenes is high-flown and rhetorical, and the action, with its threats of poisoning and stabbing, smacks of Italianate melodrama. Yet we can detect, at bottom, the same fascination with trickery that we see in the main plot: the Earl is converted by an elaborate deception – a woman who is really a man, a corpse that is not really dead. In both plots the preservation of female chastity and the discomfiture of male lust are brought about, not by earnest arguments on the moral issue, but by a series of tricks – amusing in one case, melodramatic in the other. Sex is not a matter of the soul's life and death (as in more earnest plays), but a subject on which to build amusing or exciting situations; and the final statement is that 'all is but a merriment, all but a May-game' (v.iv.278).

This formula was evidently popular, for by the following year the same writers had produced a sequel, *Northward Ho* (Paul's, 1605), in which once again moral pronouncements and trickery are blended, and sex is seen as a game with predictable rules: 'March then, this curse is on all lechers thrown, / They give horns and at last, horns are their own' (IV.i.281–2). The lecher in this case is the gallant Greenshield, who has been paying court to Mistress Mayberry, a citizen's wife. It is characteristic of his type that his main motive is not love for the woman but a desire to translate into action his cynical belief that all city wives are lecherous. When she refuses him, he is angry and incredulous:

GREENSHIELD
... if I do not take a full revenge of his wife's Puritanical coyness –
FEATHERSTONE
Suppose it she should be chaste?

GREENSHIELD

Oh, hang her; this art of seeming honest makes many of our young sons and heirs in the city, look so like our prentices – (1.i.8–12)

He takes a mean sort of revenge, pretending to Mayberry that he has actually lain with his wife, and driving the citizen to a frenzy of jealousy. But Mayberry is convinced by his wife's denial of the charge, and the rest of the action is taken up with his comic revenge on Greenshield.

The gallant's offence has been that of trying to disrupt a marriage, and the punishment is, appropriately, the disruption of his own. In chasing other women, he has neglected his own wife Kate; in fact, he regards her as something of an encumbrance, and is in the habit of referring to himself as a bachelor. Kate takes direct and appropriate action by having an affair with Featherstone, Greenshield's companion. Throughout the play, our response to this affair is one of amusement at the wife's cleverness in duping her husband – pretending, for example, that she is sleepwalking, and using this as a cover for visiting Featherstone's chamber. As one of the servants remarks, a man can take no more hold of a woman's honesty 'than of a bull 'nointed with soap, and baited with a shoal of fiddlers in Staffordshire' (III.ii.33–4). The tone is one of wry appreciation of women's knavery. And certainly there is no sympathy for the duped husband who is, we feel, merely getting what he deserves.

Featherstone plans to take Kate to Ware (location of the famous Great Bed) and lie with her there. This information comes to Mayberry's ears, and he seizes the chance to avenge himself on Greenshield by exposing his actual cuckoldry, as Greenshield pretended to expose his. This is worked in as part of a contest of practical jokes that runs through the second half of the play, and that sets the tone for Greenshield's discomfiture: it is a jest rather than a moral lecture. The gallant is made to procure Mayberry a wench for a night, little thinking that the wench (who is masked) is his own wife. When the truth is revealed he is utterly crushed; he himself cannot bear the shame he sought to inflict on Mayberry: 'I'll go instantly take a purse, be apprehended and hang'd for't, better than be a cuckold' (v.i.273–4). The comic turning of the tables is pointed out by Mayberry's friend Bellamont, who reminds Greenshield of the cuckold jokes he was going to inflict on the citizen: ' 'Twas a pretty wit of you sir, to have him rode into Puckeridge with a horn before him; ha, was't not? ... Or where a citizen keeps his house, you know 'tis not as a gentleman keeps his chamber for debt, but as you said even now very wisely, lest his horns should usher him' (v.i.256–61). There is a hint here of class revenge, of the citizen turning the tables on the gallant; but the sexual issue is the important one. Kate's adultery is presented as a laughing matter, a means of defeating her husband in the game of sex, rather like the comic revenges of *The Coxcomb* and *Jack Drum's Entertainment*.

This does not mean that the play is altogether amoral, as some critics seem to feel.[11] What it does mean is that its morality is not absolute; the strictness with which the code against adultery is applied depends on the marriage concerned. The Mayberry marriage is solid one. The ease with which the usually all-consuming passion of jealousy is killed in Mayberry indicates this; he will simply take his wife's word for it that she is chaste. And Mistress Mayberry is allowed to defend her reputation with a rhetorical passion that recalls the Earl scenes of *Westward Ho*:

> if ever I had thought unclean,
> In detestation of your nuptial pillow,
> Let sulphur drop from heaven, and nail my body
> Dead to this earth. (I.iii.100–3)

For attempting to seduce her, and for slandering her, Greenshield is unequivocally condemned. But Greenshield himself is a bad husband who deserves no loyalty, and we are made to feel more gratified than outraged when he gets none. What emerges from the play is a feeling that the moral law is not to be applied in every case alike.[12] And this open attitude is reflected in the openness of the play's dramatic mode, which allows both the amusing presentation of adultery as a good joke against a bad husband, and a straightforward dramatization of a chaste wife.

Westward Ho and *Northward Ho* are relaxed and easy-going. As in the financial intrigue comedies considered in chapter 4, the trickery is seen as an amusing game, and we are expected to take an amoral delight in the skill of the players. It so happens that the most skilful players are working for the frustration of lechery, but both plays show a casual acceptance of conventional morality rather than a deep commitment to it. The work of Thomas Middleton presents us with a different situation. He is one of the masters of intrigue comedy: his characters trick each other with a cool precision, and with an instinct for

11 Wright, *Middle-Class Culture*, pp. 630–1, claims that the play derides virtue. M.T. Jones-Davies, *Un Peintre de la vie Londonienne: Thomas Dekker* (Paris, 1958), I, 131, does not go so far, but speaks of the play's 'mœurs équivoques.'

12 A gentler and more serious assertion of the view that an erring wife can be regarded with indulgence is found in the sub-plot (generally assigned to Rowley) of Webster and Rowley's *A Cure for a Cuckold* (auspices unknown, c. 1625). The mariner Compass, returning from several years at sea to find his wife pregnant, invents humorous excuses for her, coupled with a gentle recognition that she is not a stone saint but a flesh-and-blood woman who needs to be treated with charity (II.iii); he saves his rebukes for her seducer (III.ii.43–50). The play, though a minor one, is refreshing and unusual in its balanced and charitable view of adultery.

the jugular that can be downright alarming. The casual pranksters of Dekker and Webster are, by comparison, children fighting with rubber knives. Nor is Middleton always content with a purely sporting interest in the game: he thinks – and forces us to think – about the implications of his characters' behaviour. Once again, we are confronted with the problem of how to use an intrigue comedy, with its amoral delight in the game itself, as a vehicle for moral and social commentary. And we see – as we saw in chapter 4 – that Middleton's approach to this problem, and the degree of success he achieves, vary considerably from one play to another.

In his early comedy *The Family of Love* (Admiral's? c. 1602) adultery runs riot. Practically the only characters who do not attempt or commit it are the lovers Gerardine and Maria, who, not being married, have to make do with fornication. Bedding other people's wives is a game that everyone tries to play, and the only standards that have any meaning are those of success or failure in the game. As usual, the women come off better than the men. Purge, the jealous husband of the play, tests his wife's fidelity, and finds that his suspicions are entirely justified. He attends in disguise a meeting of the Family of Love, an equivocal sect to which his wife belongs, whose gatherings are the occasion for orgies. When the lights go out he immediately offers himself to his wife (narrowly beating two gallants), and she welcomes him as a lover. But in the trial scene that ends the play, she justifies herself as Falstaff did after the Gadshill episode, claiming she knew her husband all along. There is every reason to doubt this, but she gets away with it. Though he has a legitimate reason for complaint, Purge is a loser in the game, and therefore a figure of scorn, bearing both the folly of jealousy and the shame of cuckoldry. In the final dispensing of 'justice' all he gets is a rebuke for suspecting his wife.

In citizen comedy lecherous gallants who attempt seduction generally come off badly, and Lipsalve and Gudgeon, the representatives of the type in this play, fare as badly as any. But instead of being driven off by the chastity of their intended victims, as is often the case, they are outwitted by rival and more successful lechers. They confidently assume that sex is easy to come by:

Since every place now yields a wench;
If one will not, another will:
And, if what I have heard be true,
Then young and old and all will do. (i.ii.48–51)

Or, as Lipsalve puts it more bluntly, 'more ways to the wood than one' (iii.iv.3–4). But while this may be true enough as far as the women themselves are concerned, the game is more difficult to play than they imagine. Their deepest humiliation comes at the hands of Glister; they come to him for advice on

winning Mistress Purge, and he tricks them into performing an elaborate con-
juring ritual during which they whip each other soundly. But there is no moral
force in this drubbing: they are not so much criticized for their lechery as
mocked for the folly into which lechery leads them. Certainly Glister's motives
are not those of moral correction; he resents their designs on Mistress Purge,
because he is sleeping with her himself.

The plot is not always easy to follow, but the main idea is clear: sex has little
to do with love; it has become, instead, a vehicle for the competitive instinct.
For example, Glister's wife, when she hears of his adultery, thinks only of
revenging it in kind: 'I say you are a ninnihammer, and beware the cuckoo;
for as sure as I have ware, I'll traffic with the next merchant venturer: and in
good time here comes gallants of the right trade' (v.i.27–30). The bawdy use
of commercial terms, recalling similar jokes about prostitution, shows that sex
has been dehumanized, has become a commodity. It is the means through which
the characters compete with each other. The race for Mistress Purge's favours
when the lights go out at the Family meeting is the typical event of the play.
There is no attempt at sermonizing: we simply follow and enjoy the game,
watching to see who loses and who wins. But in the sheer intensity with which
the game is played, there is a certain sardonic commentary on the characters,
who are presented as machines programmed to do only one thing. As in *Ram
Alley* and (to a lesser extent) *A Trick to Catch the Old One*, the game itself
beomes the vehicle for a satiric vision.

But Middleton was not content with this. In the subplot of *A Mad World,
my Masters* (Paul's, c. 1606) he attempts to combine the adultery intrigue with
a more overt moral commentary. This might have been easier to do if the
intrigue itself had not been so amusing, and so satisfying on its own terms.
Harebrain, the jealous husband, displays a folly and a distorted morality that
make him seem ripe for cuckolding. He locks his wife up, and tries to bully·
and frighten her into virtue:

I have convey'd away all her wanton pamphlets, as *Hero and Leander, Venus and Adon-
is*; oh, two luscious mary-bone pies for a young married wife. Here, here, prithee take
the *Resolution*, and read to her a little. ... There's a chapter of hell 'tis good to read this
cold weather. Terrify her, terrify her; go, read to her the horrible punishments for itch-
ing wantonness, the pains allotted for adultery; tell her her thoughts, her very dreams
are answerable; say so, rip up the life of a courtesan, and show how loathsome 'tis.
(1.ii.43–53)

But this speech is addressed to Frank Gullman, a courtesan, whom Harebrain
supposes to be a virtuous matron. It is perhaps a comment on his obsessive,

neurotic morality that he has unwittingly called on a courtesan to carry it out. She uses her meetings with Mistress Harebrain to plot opportunities for the latter to meet her lover Penitent Brothel. The neat irony that is one of Middleton's special skills is employed to show how Harebrain is walking into his own trap:

HAREBRAIN
Wife, as thou lov'st the quiet of my breast,
Embrace her counsel, yield to her advices;
Thou wilt find comfort in 'em in the end,
Thou'lt feel an alteration; prithee think on't.
Mine eyes can scarce refrain.
MISTRESS HAREBRAIN
Keep in your dew, sir, lest when you would, you want it.
HAREBRAIN
I've pawn'd my credit on't. Ah, didst thou know
The sweet fruit once, thou'dst never let it go.
MISTRESS HAREBRAIN
'Tis that I strive to get.
HAREBRAIN
                And still do so. (1.ii.148–56)

Gullman goes about her work with lively gusto and wit, not only contriving opportunities for Mistress Harebrain, but taking care to keep her erotically stimulated:

If he chance to steal upon you, let him find
Some book lie open 'gainst an unchaste mind,
And coted scriptures, though for your own pleasure
You read some stirring pamphlet, and convey it
Under your skirt, the fittest place to lay it. (1.ii.86–90)

But in the fourth act, after all the clever intrigue and the cheerfully bawdy dialogue, the play suddenly changes direction. We find Penitent Brothel reading a book – the sort of book that has been effectively made fun of earlier – and deeply impressed by what he reads:

Ha! Read that place again. 'Adultery
Draws the divorce 'twixt heaven and the soul.'
Accursed man, that stand'st divorc'd from heaven,
Thou wretched unthrift, that hast play'd away
Thy eternal portion at a minute's game ... (IV.i.1–5)

What follows is even more startling: a succubus appears, in the shape of Mistress Harebrain, dancing and tempting him. He drives it away with horror and loathing. This infernal vision deepens his sense of guilt, and takes us even farther from the first three acts of the play. Few critics have had a kind word to say for this succubus;[13] and both it and the scene in which it appears seem to have come from another play. Not only is the change insufficiently prepared, but the violent attack on adultery, and particularly the reading of godly books, have been effectively satirized through the presentation of Harebrain – and now Harebrain seems to be writing the play. When the three figures of the triangle are posed in a final tableau of forgiveness, love, and friendship (iv.iv.77–81), we are still rubbing our eyes in disbelief; and the rest of the play moves on to its amusing, amoral conclusion, with Frank Gullman, the chief intriguer of the adultery scenes, unrepentant and victorious in her gulling of Witgood.

The problem in *A Mad World* is that the amoral delight in intrigue and the sermons against adultery are not placed in the context of a controlling view of the subject: they both reach us at full strength, and the play splits in two. But Middleton persisted in his attempts to combine a wide range of attitudes in a single play, and in *A Chaste Maid in Cheapside* (Lady Elizabeth's c. 1613)[14] – the climax of his achievement in citizen comedy – he finally succeeded. The central situation is the arrangement by which Allwit has farmed out his wife to Sir Walter Whorehound in return for financial independence. The immoral *ménage* is so thoroughly accepted by all parties that it becomes a settled domesticity in its own right – or rather a parody of domesticity. From Allwit's point of view, it is a charitable institution run for his benefit:

The founder's come to town: I'm like a man
Finding a table furnish'd to his hand,
As mine is still to me, prays for the founder, –
'Bless the right worshipful the good founder's life.'
I thank him, 'has maintain'd my house this ten years,
Not only keeps my wife, but a keeps me

---

13 Those who have described the succubus as ineffective include Wibur D. Dunkel, *The Dramatic Technique of Thomas Middleton in his Comedies of London Life* (Chicago, 1925), p. 96, and Muriel C. Bradbrook, *The Growth and Structure of Elizabethan Comedy* (Harmondsworth, 1963), p. 168. The scene as a whole is defended by Charles A. Hallett, 'Penitent Brothel, the Succubus and Parson's *Resolution*: A Reappraisal of Penitent's Position in Middleton's Canon,' *SP*, LXIX (January 1972), 72–86; but even Hallett refers to the 'foolish antics and obvious inappropriateness' of the succubus (p. 81), differing from most other critics only in seeing the incongruity as a deliberate attempt to lighten the tone of the scene.

14 I have accepted the date proposed by R.B. Parker in his Revels edition (London, 1969), pp. xxviii–xxxv.

And all my family: I'm at his table;
He gets me all my children, and pays the nurse
Monthly or weekly; puts me to nothing,
Rent, nor church-duties, not so much as the scavenger:
The happiest state that ever man was born to! (I.ii.11–21)

As in *The Family of Love*, sex has been detached from love; here, it is simply a marketable commodity. And the Allwit *ménage* is not an isolated case: it is simply the most conspicuous symptom of a widespread sickness, in which family values are made to serve financial interest.[15] The goldsmith Yellowhammer and his wife plan to sell off their children in marriage, in exchange for money and social position: their daughter Moll to Sir Walter, and their son Tim to his 'niece' (who is really his mistress). Touchwood senior, whose amazing fertility has forced him to separate from his wife – they cannot afford a constant stream of children – sells himself as an agent of procreation to Sir Oliver and Lady Kix, whose childlessness has kept them from acquiring Sir Walter's estates. Pretending an elaborate medical treatment, he simply gets Lady Kix with child in the old-fashioned way, and is handsomely rewarded by Sir Oliver.

The brisk trade in human flesh is carried on by all parties with a combination of relish and cold-blooded precision. Allwit's speech, quoted above, is typical of the play's tone throughout the first four acts. Driven by greed, snobbery, and lust, the characters move in a series of neatly structured patterns: they even see themselves as players in a game. In the last act Sir Walter, defeated and despairing, leaves the stage with the words: 'If ever eyes were open, these are they: / Gamesters, farewell, I have nothing left to play' (v.i.148–9), while Allwit, who has come out not too badly, accepts the risks of the game with a cheerful flippancy: 'There's no gamester like a politic sinner, / For whoe'er games, the box is sure a winner' (v.i.167–8). To some extent, the characters' delight in their own inventiveness communicates itself to us; like Middleton's earlier work, the play gives the amoral pleasure of a skilfully worked out comedy of intrigue. But while we appreciate the skill of the players, our appreciation is qualified. For one thing, there is no one central intriguer – like Frank Gullman in *A Mad World* – who is obviously ahead in the game, and who can win the audience's admiration on that basis. The characters exude vitality and self-confidence; they congratulate themselves on the success or imminent success of their plans; but they are never so much masters of their situations as they

---

15 See Samuel Schoenbaum, '*A Chaste Maid in Cheapside* and Middleton's City Comedy,' in *Studies in the English Renaissance Drama*, ed. Josephine W. Bennett *et all*. (New York, 1959), p. 293; and Ruby Chatterji, 'Theme, Imagery, and Unity in *A Chaste Maid In Cheapside*,' *Renaissance Drama*, VIII (1965), pp. 106–16.

think they are. We have seen how Allwit congratulates himself on his financial independence, but in giving up his responsibilities he has also given up his authority. His servants refer to Sir Walter as their master, and treat Allwit with contempt: 'O, you are but / Our mistress's husband' (1.ii.61–2). Sir Walter does not even allow him to go to bed with his own wife (1.ii.94–6). The servants sneer at him for having given up his sex life: 'Now's out of work, he falls to making dildoes' (1.ii.58). As if that were not enough, he has come to depend so much on the continuance of Sir Walter's favours that any threat of their removal can reduce him to panic, and can be used against him as blackmail (1.ii.96–103). In short, his sense of freedom is an illusion; he is in many respects the most enslaved character in the play.

Similar ironies affect the other characters. Sir Walter has so thoroughly consolidated his position as Mistress Allwit's lover that he has lost all the independence of a lover and taken on the worries and responsibilities of a husband – including jealousy. In Allwit's words,

> he's jealous for me,
> Watches her steps, sets spies; I live at ease,
> He has both the cost and torment. (1.ii.52–4)

The Yellowhammers hope for riches from connecting their family with Sir Walter's (1.i.129). In point of fact, it is Sir Walter who hopes to gain financially (11.i.155–6); each party preys on the other, and neither seems to notice that the other is preying on him. The result of all this is that the audience's delight in a game well played – a delight that can break down moral judgments in an intrigue comedy – is never allowed to develop fully, since none of the major players is as clever as he thinks he is. The most successful players are the Touchwood brothers, who are acting out of motives with which the audience would normally sympathize in any case. Touchwood junior and Moll Yellowhammer are in love, and want to frustrate the mercenary match her parents have arranged. Touchwood senior, though he sells himself to the Kixes, does so to support his wife and family, to whom he is genuinely devoted (11.i.1–6). But in contemplating Sir Walter, the Allwits, and the Yellowhammers, we are not encouraged to take sides, as we are, I think, in the early scenes of A Mad World, my Masters.

The way remains clear, then, for a critical judgment of the main characters. In the first four acts, the commentary is largely sardonic, and (as in Michaelmas Term) it is most effective when it is made implicitly, through the imagery.[16]

---

16 See Schoenbaum, 'Chaste Maid,' p. 300, and Chatterji, 'Theme, Imagery, and Unity,' pp. 118–25.

Human beings are described in terms that reduce them to beasts, inanimate objects, or salable commodities. Allwit, describing his source of income, says that he thrives 'As other trades thrive, butchers by selling flesh, / Poulters by vending conies, or the like, coz' (iv.i.216–17). This idea is dramatized in ii.ii., when the Country Wench casually disposes of an unwanted baby by pretending it is a piece of meat. Sir Walter says to his mistress, 'I bring thee up to turn thee into gold, wench' (i.i.100). When Moll Yellowhammer seems on the point of death, her brother's words reflect the way her parents had intended to use her: 'Chang'd? Gold into white money was never so chang'd / As is my sister's colour into paleness' (v.ii.16–17). Such statements are amusing up to a point, through their cool impudence, but they also bring into focus our sense of unease at the way these people dehumanize each other.

Then in the last act there is an explicit, moralizing denunciation of vice, of the sort that wrecked the balance of *Michaelmas Term* and *A Mad World, my Masters*. Sir Walter, wounded by Touchwood junior, is brought back to the Allwits' house, where he denounces both them and himself for immorality:

Thou know'st me to be wicked, for thy baseness
Kept the eyes open still on all my sins;
None knew the dear account my soul stood charg'd with
So well as thou, yet, like hell's flattering angel,
Would'st never tell me on't, let'st me go on,
And join with death in sleep; that if I had not
Wak'd now by chance, even by a stranger's pity,
I had everlastingly slept out all hope
Of grace and mercy.
...
O, how my offences wrestle with my repentance!
It hath scarce breath;
Still my adulterous guilt hovers aloft,
And with her black wings beats down all my prayers
Ere they be half way up. What's he knows now
How long I have to live? O, what comes then?
My taste grows bitter; the round world all gall now;
Her pleasing pleasures now hath poison'd me,
Which I exchang'd my soul for:
Make way a hundred sighs at once for me! (v.i.23–31, 72–81)

The change of tone is startling, but this time the ground has been prepared for it, and it extends the play's range without tearing it apart.[17] The restraint of our appreciation of the characters' wit, and the sardonic commentary on the debasing of human values, have prevented us from being fully committed to the amoral pleasures of the game. In the scene by the Thames, shortly before Sir Walter's outburst, we have seen Mistress Yellowhammer drag Moll away from her lover with such brutality that even the watermen, anonymous background figures, protest (iv.iv.19–23); this darkens the tone of the play, and aids the transition to a new moral earnestness. Sir Walter himself has joined in the protest, and this too helps to prepare us for his new role.[18]

Most important, however, is the fact that Sir Walter's tirade – unlike Penitent Brothel's vision of guilt – is not allowed to have *too* much effect. Sir Walter remains the only penitent, and his remorse is played off against Allwit's continuing, incorrigible cynicism. When it becomes apparent that the knight's usefulness is at an end, Allwit orders him out of the house, with a speech that would be hard to match for sheer breathtaking audacity:

> I must tell you, sir,
> You have been somewhat bolder in my house
> Than I could well like of; I suffer'd you
> Till it stuck here at my heart; I tell you truly
> I thought you had been familiar with my wife once. (v.i.141–5)

After 'the founder' has been carried off, the Allwits calmly take stock of their gains, decide they are quite well off, and determine to let out lodgings. The Yellowhammers come out even: their son (they discover too late) has married a whore, but their daughter has made a respectable if not a glittering match, and they are content. Sir Oliver Kix awards Touchwood senior a permanent appointment as a fertility agent – 'Get children, and I'll keep them' (v.iv.76) – suggesting that the Allwit game is about to begin again, with a different set of players.[19] Only Sir Walter is thoroughly penitent, and only Sir Walter is thoroughly crushed – an ironic reversal of the normal comic ending, in which repentant characters are rewarded with a comfortable maintenance. The play's

17 For a contrary opinion, see T.B. Tomlinson, *A Study of Elizabethan and Jacobean Tragedy* (Cambridge, 1964), pp. 165–6. Tomlinson feels that the transition almost works, but that the tone of Sir Walter's long speech 'is certainly a mistake on Middleton's part.'

18 David M. Holmes has suggested that Sir Walter's conversion is also anticipated by his generosity to his Welsh mistress, and his contempt for Allwit. See *The Art of Thomas Middleton* (Oxford, 1970), pp. 94–5.

19 See Robert I. Williams, 'Machiavelli's *Mandragola*, Touchwood Senior, and the Comedy of Middleton's *A Chaste Maid in Cheapside*,' *SEL*, x (Spring 1970), 392–3.

vision includes Sir Walter's moral revulsion; but it also includes a sardonic recognition that no amount of preaching can change a world as corrupt as this one. An interesting indication of this is that Yellowhammer is allowed to speak the last lines of the play, a function usually reserved for sympathetic or reformed characters. His two children have just been married, and 'the best is, / One feast will serve them both' (v.iv.114–15). Money counts, right up to the final curtain.

Middleton, then, has finally brought together the three main strands of his comic vision – an amoral delight in his characters' skill, satiric joking about the world they inhabit, and finally moral revulsion – and interwoven them in a way that gives each one its due, but keeps them in balance. But we are still aware of each element as potentially separate, and of the sheer effort required to preserve the harmony among them. Ben Jonson's special gift, as we saw in discussing *The Alchemist*, is to make such a balance seem natural. In *The Devil is an Ass* (King's, 1616) the wit of the adultery game, laughter at the folly of a husband, and a firm assertion of the necessity of chastity are all pulled together into a tight dramatic unit. The controlling factor is not a casual inclusiveness, as in Dekker and Webster, or a painstaking effort to keep warring impulses under control, as in Middleton, but a critical analysis that is searching enough to see all sides of the question, and rigorous enough to make a positive statement at the end.

We are presented with the usual triangle of seducer, chaste wife, and jealous husband, and it is the last of these who takes up much of our attention in the early scenes. The jealousy of Fitzdottrel is not a simple obsession, but part of the comic confusion of values that dominates his character. His greed for money and social position; his willingness to fall in with the most fantastic schemes, if he thinks they will further his ambitions; his childish desire to see the devil, to whom, despite his jealousy, he is prepared to sacrifice even his wife – all this indicates a mind whose sense of proportion is virtually non-existent. Fitzdottrel's jealousy is laughable, but, as so often in Jonson, the laughter is based not on obvious, predictable jokes, but on an exact sense of the character's folly. Telling his servant not to let anyone in, he shows himself suspicious of the most innocent items, and reluctant to show the most ordinary courtesies; his attitude to the common things of life is distorted by his folly:

> nor no youths, disguis'd
> Like country wives, with cream, and marrow-puddings.
> Much knavery may be vented in a pudding,
> Much bawdy intelligence; they are shrewd ciphers.

Nor turn the key to any neighbour's need,
Be't but to kindle fire, or beg a little,
Put it out, rather; all out, to an ash,
That they may see no smoke. (II.i.164–71)

He treats his wife not as a woman to be loved, but as a possession to be locked up. He dresses her up as one would do a tailor's dummy, to satisfy his own self-esteem, and expects her to be grateful for this (II.vii.28–41). One of his first actions in the play is to loan her out for fifteen minutes' conversation, in return for a rich cloak. To him she is simply a commodity.[20] The irony is that he is trying to prevent other men from enjoying what he does not properly enjoy himself. Her lover Wittipol speaks of 'The cold / Sheets that you lie in, with the watching candle' (I.vi. 91–2) which are all she has in the evenings, while her husband wanders abroad, trying to conjure the devil.

It could be argued – and indeed Wittipol does argue – that such a husband deserves cuckolding. And one feels this more strongly in that Wittipol himself is not (like Greenshield in *Northward Ho* or Lord Beaufort in *Anything for a Quiet Life*) the sort of cynical, maladroit lecher who is usually set in opposition to the chaste woman. For once the seducer is genuinely attractive. His plea to the lady to make use of her beauty while there is still time is expressed with lyric grace:

> Think,
> All beauty doth not last until the autumn.
> You grow old, while I tell you this. (I.vi.129–31)

The idea may be a poetic commonplace, but the simple truth with which Wittipol expresses it catches us by surprise. He pays tribute to the lady's beauty in a speech that has the charm and delicacy of Jonson's best love songs and that, in fact, concludes with one of those songs, the exquisite lyric whose second verse begins, 'Have you seen but a bright lily grow' (II.vi.94–113). Wittipol has also a sense of propriety and honour. In the scene in which he and Mistress Fitzdottrel speak to each other from neighbouring windows, he assures her that his friend Manly has tactfully retired: 'Neither need you doubt him, / If he were here. He is too much a gentleman' (II.vi.47–8). When she actually falls into his hands, he tells her,

---

20 In this he resembles Corvino in *Volpone*, who treats Celia as a possession to be locked up, or loaned out, as his self-interest dictates: 'What, is my gold / The worse for touching? clothes, for being look'd on? / Why, this's no more' (III.vii.40–2).

Be not afraid, sweet lady; you are trusted
To love, not violence here; I am no ravisher,
But one, whom you, by your fair trust again,
May of a servant make a most true friend. (IV.vi. 1–4)

Furthermore, their minds work together effectively: she has her own wit, and it is through her cleverness (and his quickness in responding to her suggestions) that their crucial meeting is arranged.

But our response to Wittipol's courtship becomes increasingly hedged about with reservations. His intrigue becomes tangled with the shabby trickery of the projector Meercraft, and while Wittipol tries to keep his dignity, the association taints him slightly; moreover, the idea of adultery is deglamourised by the coarse and stupid sensuality of Lady Tailbush and Lady Eitherside. Most important, Mistress Fitzdottrel herself, though no meek, submissive wife, sees that adultery is not the answer to her problem. Having noted the nobility of Wittipol, and the wit he displays in gaining access to her, she appeals to these qualities as the basis for a different relationship, based on honesty. She grants her husband's folly, but it is more important to her to have Wittipol's friendship to help control it than his body to avenge it:

'Tis counsel that I want, and honest aids:
And in this name, I need you, for a friend,
Never in any other; for his ill,
Must not make me, sir, worse. (IV.vi.25–8)

What she proposes is, in fact, more consonant with Wittipol's high-minded disposition than adultery would have been, and Wittipol, urged by Manly, accepts her offer.

The one safeguard Fitzdottrel would not trust – his wife's natural honesty – has saved his brows from horns when all his frantic efforts to keep her and Wittipol apart have failed. Jonson has presented a situation in which one might have been sympathetic to adultery: a woman, shackled to a bad husband, is tempted by an attractive and virtuous lover. But the situation also makes the defeat of adultery both possible and desirable: it would be a pity if a man of Wittipol's fine instincts were permitted to sin, and those instincts provide the opportunity of saving him. The transition from sensual love to honest friendship springs easily from what we know of the character's better nature,[21] and the new relationship is more directly useful to Mistress Fitzdottrel in her trou-

---

21 See C.G.Thayer, *Ben Jonson: Studies in the Plays* (Norman, Oklahoma, 1963), p. 164.

bles than simple adultery would be. Jonson also tackles the problem of a convincing resolution for the wife's relationship with her husband. The conventional repentance and reconciliation would not work here; Fitzdottrel is such a deep-dyed fool and knave that the best one can hope for is his defeat. This comes with the comic appropriateness that distinguishes Jonson at his best. His snobbery makes him court the cuckoldry he fears, for he hands his wife over to what he thinks is a fine lady (really Wittipol in disguise) with the words, 'She is your own. Do with her what you will!' (IV.iv.253). Once the truth has been revealed, his jealousy punishes itself; he cannot accept the assurances of the other characters, but remains convinced that he has been cuckolded. Meanwhile, through the disguise, Wittipol and Manly gain control over his estate, a control they intend to use to protect the wife from her husband's folly. The honourable alliance of wife and lover produces results almost as soon as it is made. As he did in *The Alchemist*, Jonson has provided an ending which fits our responses to the characters throughout: our sympathies have been engaged both for wit and for high-mindedness, and each wins its own victory, in the defeat of Fitzdottrel and the preservation of the lovers' virtue.

Jonson's firm critical intelligence keeps his play under control; the audience's approval and disapproval are carefully measured and carefully directed. A similar feat of control is found in Shakespeare's only citizen comedy, *The Merry Wives of Windsor* (Chamberlain's, 1597). Here, the presentation is so light and urbane that we are hardly aware of watching a moral comedy; and yet its moral structure is as firm as Jonson's. The play is easily undervalued, since it stands apart from the rest of the canon, and comparison with Shakespeare's other work does not show it to advantage; but comparison with other citizen comedies may show that its blending of moral assertion with a delight in trickery commands respect, and that even in a genre he touched only once Shakespeare set standards that his contemporaries found hard to match.

The basic situation is simple and familiar. Two chaste wives repel a seducer, and shame a jealous husband; but the assertion of chastity is achieved without preaching, and in a spirit of fun. Mistress Ford and Mistress Page react to their dilemmas, not with the sober patience of wives in more conventional plays, but with sharp wit and lively indignation – caustic remarks about the lechery of men, spirited vows of revenge, and, most significant of all, highly coloured descriptions of Falstaff's physical grotesqueness. The latter provides a comic equivalent for the moral indignation felt at the idea of adultery. Mistress Page's speech, on receiving Falstaff's form letter of courtship, is typical: 'I warrant he hath a thousand of these letters, writ with blank space for different names – sure, more – and these are of the second edition. He will print them, out of doubt; for he cares not what he puts into the press, when he would put us two:

I had rather be a giantess, and lie under Mount Pelion. Well, I will find you twenty lascivious turtles ere one chaste man' (II.i.71–8).

With their outrage expressing itself thus, in amusing comments about Falstaff's fat, it is appropriate that the punishments they devise should be designed to mortify the flesh – quite literally. As Mistress Ford puts it, 'I think the best way were to entertain him with hope till the wicked fire of lust have melted him in his own grease' (II.i.64–6). Falstaff, by his own admission, is certainly melted in his own grease in the buck-basket, and his subsequent immersion poses another threat: 'I had been drowned but that the shore was shelvy and shallow – a death that I abhor: for the water swells a man; and what a thing should I have been when I had been swelled! I should have been a mountain of mummy' (III.v.13–17). Later, he is beaten black and blue by Ford's cudgel, and burned with tapers, which may signify in their small way the 'fires of lust' that Mistress Ford hoped would consume him.

The practical jokes, amusing in themselves, are also appropriate comic punishments. But the victim of the jokes has a certain resilience, which ensures that not all the laughter is against him. He is no mere punching-bag as are, for example, Lipsalve and Gudgeon in *The Family of Love*. For one thing, he is not a helpless victim of love, or even of lust: his vanity is tickled by the favourable response to his letters, but when he says, 'they say the jealous wittolly knave hath masses of money, for the which his wife seems to me well-favoured' (II.ii.260–2), there is no doubt where his priorities lie. For him, the affair is largely a commercial venture, and he goes about it with enough wit to score a few points of his own. Moreover, some of his finest displays of wit come when he is reacting to his failures:

I suffered the pangs of three several deaths. First, an intolerable fright, to be detected with a jealous rotten bell-wether; next, to be compassed like a good bilbo in the circumference of a peck, hilt to point, heel to head; and then to be stopped in like a strong distillation with stinking clothes that fretted in their own grease – think of that – a man of my kidney – think of that – that am as subject to heat as butter; a man of continual dissolution and thaw: it was a miracle to 'scape suffocation. And in the height of this bath, when I was more than half stewed in grease, like a Dutch dish, to be thrown into the Thames and cooled, glowing hot, in that surge, like a horse-shoe – think of that – hissing hot – think of that, Master Brook! (III.v.98–113)

In a sense, the victim of the jest has had the last laugh after all, for in describing his discomfiture he produces a triumph of wit. Though he has been put – lightly, but firmly – in his place, the old rogue still wins our appreciative laughter.

The treatment of Ford, the jealous husband, is also carefully balanced. A jealous husband who tries to confirm his suspicions by paying another man to seduce his wife could be simply an unpleasant, melodramatic villain – like Sir John Loveall in *Amends for Ladies*. And some critics have taken a dark view of Ford: H.C. Hart calls him 'nauseous – a nasty pill,'[22] and Thomas Marc Parrott refers to him as a 'dark figure,' whose passion is 'not far removed from the tragic.'[23] But while a dispassionate analysis of his intentions might produce such a reaction, the play presents him in quite a different light. A man with an obsession can be frightening, or silly, or both. Ford, for the most part, is silly. His language remains on the level of prosaic exasperation, and his actions end in comic futility, as he searches empty houses and empty buck-baskets, following one wild-goose chase after another. Like Falstaff, Ford is put in his place, but in a light and comic way, and no serious indignation is roused against him.

The play concludes with the final deluding of Falstaff in Windsor Forest. He is made, with ironic appropriateness, to wear horns; emblematically speaking, he suffers the fate he had hoped to inflict on Ford and Page. The horns, and the 'noise of hunting' which scatters the fairies, also suggest a comic version of the Actaeon myth, representing the punishment of lust.[24] The villagers' performance, in fact, is rather like a Masque of Chastity: Falstaff is tested by the fairies and found sinful. He is pinched and burned, while the fairies rebuke him (in song) for his sins (v.v.94–103). This provides a final, and formal, theatrical expression of the play's morality. But even here, the balance is maintained, and the Windsor citizens are not allowed an unqualified triumph. There are ironies in the masque itself. The casting of Mistress Quickly as the Fairy Queen adds a tongue-in-cheek quality to the masque's expression of morality: this enthusiastic go-between is hardly the person to lecture Falstaff on his sins.[25] And the masque is also used as a cover for Fenton's capture of Anne Page, in

22 Introduction to the (Old) Arden edition (London, 1904), p. lv
23 *Shakespearean Comedy* (New York, 1949), p. 270
24 See John M. Steadman, 'Falstaff as Actaeon: A Dramatic Emblem,' *SQ*, xiv (Summer 1963), 231–44.
25 Hart ([Old] Arden intro., p. xlii) is, in fact, extremely distressed by this unconventional piece of casting and hopefully suggests a textual error. Fenton (iv.vi.20) and Mistress Page (iv.iv.70) both say that Anne will play the Fairy Queen, and some editors follow this suggestion. The Quarto quite definitely identifies Mistress Quickly as the Fairy Queen in the stage direction for the fairies' entrance. The Folio's stage direction is a simple 'Enter Fairies,' and some of the speech headings for the Queen are 'Qu.'; others are 'Qui.' The possibility that 'Qui.' here is an unwarranted expansion of 'Qu.' in the manuscript, together with the evidence of Fenton and Mistress Page, constitute the case for Anne. But most editors prefer Mistress Quickly. This is reasonable textually (there are so many small plot confusions that Fenton's and Mistress Page's evidence should not be too strictly applied) and produces, I think, a more interesting and significant effect.

which her parents' attempt to force her into marrying their own choice of suitors is frustrated. Just as the triumphant citizens are heaping insults on Falstaff, they discover that they have been defeated on another front. One can see Falstaff's eyes light up: 'I am glad, though you have ta'en a special stand to strike at me, that your arrow hath glanced' (v.v.231–2). In the end, honours are about even, and the play ends with a tableau of forgiveness, in which the Pages welcome their new son-in-law, the wives invite their would-be seducer into their homes for a more innocent purpose, and the jealous husband is reconciled with his wife:

PAGE
Well, what remedy? Fenton, heaven give thee joy!
What cannot be eschew'd must be embrac'd.

FALSTAFF
When night-dogs run, all sorts of deer are chas'd.

MRS. PAGE
Well, I will muse no further. Master Fenton,
Heaven give you many, many merry days!
Good husband, let us every one go home,
And laugh this sport o'er by a country fire,
Sir John and all.

FORD
                    Let it be so. – Sir John,
To Master Brook you yet shall hold your word,
For he to-night shall lie with Mistress Ford. (v.v.233–42)

The note of reconciliation rings true enough; one even takes it for granted. But looking back over other comedies in which marriages are challenged and disrupted, one sees that such endings are not so easy to bring off. The reconciliations in *Anything for a Quiet Life* and *A Mad World, my Masters* were forced, unconvincingly, on situations where the tensions seemed too great to disappear so easily; and in the plays of Dekker and Webster some real misconduct was quickly glossed over. The endings of *A Chaste Maid in Cheapside* and *The Devil is an Ass* were convincing precisely because they did not attempt too much. But Shakespeare has judged his characters lightly, keeping his morality clear but not insisting too heavily on its importance. As a result of this balance, vice is clearly seen for what it is, yet reconciliation comes naturally. Though it has neither the satiric bite nor the moral urgency of other comedies of adultery, *The Merry Wives of Windsor* is as fundamentally serious as any of the plays we have discussed, and its treatment of the game of sex is amusing, judicious, and humane.

8
Conclusion

Seen from the perspective set up by reference books, the term 'citizen comedy' too often conveys only a vague, general impression of usurers cheating prodigals, gallants sleeping with citizens' wives, and merry shopkeepers becoming Lord Mayors of London. A closer acquaintance with the genre, however, shows the plays as varied and unpredictable, employing a wide range of conventions and attitudes, and providing considerable scope for the peculiarities of individual writers. Within this variety, a certain pattern of tension can be discerned, and it is a pattern that reveals something basic about comedy itself. The drive to the happy ending usually involves a cementing of the social order: marriages are made (or restored after a period of disruption); property is restored to its owner; a building is erected; a banquet is given. This kind of ending generally involves a defence of the conventional moral standards regarding money, marriage, and sex. Within the structure of comedy there is also scope, and even encouragement, for the fulfilment of individual desires. When the prodigal gets his land back, or the lover gets his girl, the interests of the individual and of society are finally identical. But this is not always the case. The cheater who is out for private gain, the rake who is seeking his own pleasures – these can appeal to an audience by the wit and flair with which they overturn respectability. When this happens, we see in the standards of conventional morality not security and reassurance, but killjoy restriction.

The assertion of morality and the subversion of morality are the poles between which citizen comedy moves. The tensions of individual plays, and the variety of the genre as a whole, result from the writers' attempts to work out their own solutions to this underlying tension in the medium. We saw in the last chapter how much the results depend on the talent and temperament of the individual playwright – a factor that is finally more important than the difference between public and private theatres, or between one decade and another. It is as though the impulses that produced Restoration comedy and those that produced Sentimental comedy were present in equal force in the same set of writers. But a reference to these later developments may remind us that comedy has frequently been created from a tension of opposing values. Congreve's *Love for Love* is in the Restoration tradition, yet the hero's attempts to win the girl through wit and trickery fail; he succeeds in the Sentimental manner, through a display of generosity and good nature. In *The School for Scandal*, Sheridan attacks the excesses of Sentimental comedy but preserves its concern with moral testing and the rewards of virtue. Shaw's *Arms and the Man* is a self-proclaimed 'anti-romantic comedy' in which all the old romantic devices are brazenly employed, and the practical hero professes himself, in the end, an incurable romantic. Looking back to Shakespearean comedy, we recognize a similar tension between a witty scepticism about romantic love and a final admission of its power. Comedy is concerned simultaneously with mockery and with defence, and while this sometimes produces a simple pattern of sympathies – when, for example, a usurer is frustrated and a love-match achieved – there are many cases where the value mocked and the value defended are the same.

Citizen comedy in the period under discussion is concerned with social relations in their most material form – sex and marriage, money and property. The same interests persist in later comedy, of course, but writers like Congreve and Wilde also show a concern for more delicate social adjustments – such as the right degree of seriousness for a profession of love – that we do not find in the earlier plays. The characters of citizen comedy are too close to the sources of their security, and too anxious about them, to have any time for such niceties. The result is a comedy coarser in texture than its successors, displaying an urgent concern for the material side of life, and often for little else. Its social morality is finally a morality of property and possession. Each man should keep and use what is rightfully his, whether his land or his wife: the moralizing comedies rebuke the neglect of wives and the squandering of wealth in roughly similar terms. A woman's chastity, likewise, is her dearest possession, and is not to be squandered. In writers as different as Jonson and Dekker we see a concern for the preservation of chastity and the right use of wealth – and beneath it all, a concern for the stability of society.

But too exclusive a concern with stability and preservation can lead to meanness of spirit. The cheaters who deal in money and the whores who deal in sex may be out for themselves, but they are also keeping the traffic of life moving, keeping society from atrophy. In their attacks on respectability, we recognize an amoral energy that, whatever else we may think of it, keeps social life lively and challenging. And it is a force we must understand if we are to understand the world we live in: we may not want to *live* in Bartholomew Fair, but it is unwise not to visit it from time to time. As Shakespeare's comedies balance our attitudes to romantic love, showing both its value and its limits, the citizen comedies of his contemporaries, seen as a whole, balance our attitudes to social stability. Individual plays may come down on one side or another, but the major writers – Jonson, Middleton, Marston, Dekker, and on one occasion Shakespeare – are aware of the broader possibilities of the form, and show that the security of the community and the desires of the individual both deserve respect; that on occasion they can be harmonized; and that when they cannot, it is part of the business of comedy to see that one does not crush the other. This breadth of vision is not always easy to express in dramatic terms, and it produced some unstable plays; but it also produced *The Alchemist, Eastward Ho*, and *The Merry Wives of Windsor*, to name only three of many successes, and the genre as a whole, with its lively examination of man the social animal, has more than an antiquarian claim on our attention.

Selected bibliography

EDITIONS OF PLAYS

Armin, Robert. *The Two Maids of More-clacke*. London, 1609
Barry, David Lord. *Ram Alley*. See Dodsley
Beaumont, Francis and John Fletcher. *The Coxcomb, The Knight of the Burning Pestle*, and *The Scornful Lady*. In *The Dramatic Works in the Beaumont and Fletcher Canon*, Vols. I–II, ed. Fredson Bowers. Cambridge, 1966, 1970
– *The Night Walker, Wit at Several Weapons*, and *Wit Without Money*. In *The Works of Francis Beaumont and John Fletcher*, ed. Arnold Glover and A.R. Waller. 10 vols. Cambridge, 1905–12
Brooke, C.F. Tucker, ed. *The Shakespeare Apocrypha*. Oxford, 1908. Contains *The London Prodigal, The Merry Devil of Edmonton*, and *The Puritan*
Chapman, George. *Eastward Ho* (with Jonson and Marston). See Jonson
Club Law, ed. G.C. Moore Smith. Cambridge, 1907
Cooke, Jo. *Greene's Tu Quoque*. See Dodsley
Davenport, Robert. *A New Trick to Cheat the Devil*. In *Old English Plays*, New Series, Vol. III: *The Works of Robert Davenport*, ed. A.H. Bullen. New York, 1964
Dekker, Thomas. *The Honest Whore, Part One* (with Middleton) and *Part Two, Northward Ho* (with Webster), *The Roaring Girl* (with Middleton), *The Shoemakers' Holiday*, and *Westward Ho* (with Webster). In *The Dramatic Works of Thomas Dekker*, ed. Fredson Bowers. 4 vols. Cambridge, 1953–61
Dodsley, Robert, ed. *A Select Collection of Old English Plays*, 4th ed., rev. by W. Carew Hazlitt. 15 vols. London, 1874–6. Contains Barry, *Ram Alley*;

Cooke, *Greene's Tu Quoque*; Haughton, *Grim the Collier of Croydon*; *How a Man May Choose a Good Wife From a Bad*; Rowley, *A Match at Midnight* and *A New Wonder, a Woman Never Vexed*; and Tailor, *The Hog Hath Lost his Pearl*

The Fair Maid of Bristow, ed. Arthur Hobson Quinn. Philadelphia, 1902

The Fair Maid of the Exchange (Malone Society Reprint). Oxford, 1962

Field, Nathan. *Amends for Ladies* and *A Woman is a Weather-cock*. In *The Plays of Nathan Field*, ed. William Peery. Austin, Texas, 1950

Fletcher, John. *The Woman's Prize*, ed. George B. Ferguson. The Hague, 1966. See also Beaumont and Fletcher

Haughton, William. *Englishmen for my Money* (Malone Society Reprint). Oxford, 1912

- *Grim the Collier of Croydon*. See Dodsley

Heywood, Thomas. *If You Know Not Me, You Know Nobody, Part Two* and *The Wise-woman of Hogsdon*. In *The Dramatic Works of Thomas Heywood*. ed. R.H. Shepherd. 6 vols. London, 1874

How A Man May Choose a Good Wife From a Bad. See Dodsley

Jonson, Ben. *The Alchemist, Bartholomew Fair, The Devil is an Ass, Eastward Ho* (with Chapman and Marston), *Epicoene, Every Man in his Humour, Every Man out of his Humour, The Staple of News*, and *A Tale of a Tub*. In *Ben Jonson*, ed. C.H. Herford and Percy and Evelyn Simpson. 11 vols. Oxford, 1925–52

The London Prodigal. See Brooke

Marston, John. *The Dutch Courtesan*, ed. M.L. Wine (Regents Renaissance Drama Series). Lincoln, Nebraska, 1965

- *Eastward Ho* (with Chapman and Jonson). See Jonson

- *Jack Drum's Entertainment*. In *The Plays of John Marston*, ed. H. Harvey Wood. 3 vols. Edinburgh, 1934–9

Massinger, Philip. *A New Way to Pay Old Debts*, ed. T.W. Craik (New Mermaids). London, 1964

The Merry Devil of Edmonton. See Brooke

Middleton, Thomas. *Anything for a Quiet Life* (with Webster?). In *The Complete Works of John Webster*, ed. F.L. Lucas. 4 vols. London, 1927

- *A Chaste Maid in Cheapside*, ed. R.B. Parker (Revels Plays). London, 1969

- *A Fair Quarrel* (with Rowley), *The Family of Love, No Wit, No Help, Like a Woman's*, and *Your Five Gallants*. In *The Works of Thomas Middleton*, ed. A.H. Bullen. 8 vols. London, 1885–6

- *The Honest Whore, Part One* and *The Roaring Girl* (with Dekker). See Dekker

- *A Mad World, My Masters*, ed. Standish Henning (Regents Renaissance Drama Series). Lincoln, Nebraska, 1965

– *Michaelmas Term*, ed. Richard Levin (Regents Renaissance Drama Series). Lincoln, Nebraska, 1966

– *A Trick to Catch the Old One*, ed. Charles Barber (Fountainwell Drama Texts). Edinburgh, 1968

Percy, William. *The Cuck-queans and Cuckolds Errants*, ed. John Arthur Lloyd. London, 1824

Porter, Henry. *The Two Angry Women of Abington*. In *Nero and Other Plays*, ed. Havelock Ellis *et al.* (Mermaid edition). London, 1888

The Puritan. See Brooke

Rowley, William. *A Cure for a Cuckold* (with Webster). In *The Complete Works of John Webster*, ed. F.L. Lucas. 4 vols. London, 1927

– *A Fair Quarrel* (with Middleton). See Middleton

– *A Match at Midnight* and *A New Wonder, a Woman Never Vexed*. See Dodsley

S.,S. *The Honest Lawyer.* London, 1616

Shakespeare, William. *The Merry Wives of Windsor*, ed. H.J. Oliver (The Arden Shakespeare). London, 1971

Sharpham, Edward. *Cupid's Whirligig.* London, 1607

– *The Fleer.* London, 1607

Tailor, Robert. *The Hog hath Lost his Pearl.* See Dodsley

Webster, John. *Anything for a Quiet Life* (with Middleton). See Middleton

– *A Cure for a Cuckold* (with Rowley). See Rowley

– *Northward Ho* and *Westward Ho* (with Dekker). See Dekker

Wily Beguiled (Malone Society Reprint). Oxford, 1912

SOCIAL COMMENTARY BY CONTEMPORARIES OF THE PLAYWRIGHTS

Note: This section includes modern compilations of material from the period. London is the place of publication, unless otherwise stated.

A. *The Passionate Morrice*, ed. F.J. Furnivall. New Shakspere Society, Series VI, no. 2. 1878

'Anger, Jane.' *Jane Anger her Protection for Women* ... 1589

Aylett, Robert. *The Brides Ornaments* ... 1625

– *Thrift's Eqvipage* ... 1622

B., Ste. *Covnsel to the Hvsband: to the Wife Instruction* ... 1608

Bacon, Francis. *Essays*, ed. F.G. Selby. 1958

Becon, Thomas. *The Booke of Matrimony* ... In *The worckes of T. Becon, whiche he hath hytherto made and published.* 1560

Brathwait, Richard. *Ar't asleepe Husband? A Boulster Lecture* ... 1640

– *The English Gentleman.* 1630

– *The English Gentlewoman* ... 1631

Breton, Nicholas. *The Good and the Badde.* 1616
– *A Poste With a Packet of Madde Letters.* 1605
Bullinger, Heinrich. *The Christian State of Matrimonye* ... tr. Miles Coverdale. 1541
Chappell, William, ed. *The Roxburgh Ballads.* Vols. I–III. Hertford, 1869–79
Cleaver, Robert. *A godlie forme of hovseholde government* ... 1598. (Note: There were two editions published in that year, and they differ considerably from each other. The one referred to is STC 5383)
Dekker, Thomas. *The Seven deadly Sins of London*, ed. Edward Arber. Westminster, 1895
Deloney, Thomas. *Works*, ed. F.O. Mann. Oxford, 1912
Dent, Arthur. *The Plaine Man's Path-way to Heauen* ... 1601
Ferrers, Richard. *The Worth of Women.* 1622
G.,I. *An Apologie for Women-Kinde.* 1605
Gibbon, Charles. *A Work worth the Reading* ... 1591
Gibson, Anthony. *A womans woorth* ... 1599
Greene, Robert. *Penelopes Web.* 1587
Harrison, G.B., ed. *The Elizabethan Journals.* 1955
– *A Jacobean Journal.* 1946
– *A Second Jacobean Journal.* 1958
Harrison, William. *The Description of England*, ed. Georges Edelen. Ithaca, N.Y., 1968
Heywood, Thomas. *A Curtaine Lectvre* ... 1638
– *Gunaikeion* ... 1624
Hill, Robert. *The Pathway to Prayer, and Pietie* ... 1610
Johnson, Richard. *Look on me London* ... 1613
– *The Pleasant Walkes of Moore-fields.* 1607
Latimer, Hugh. *Fruitfull Sermons Preached by the right reuerend Father, and constant Martyr of Iesus Christ M. Hugh Latimer* ... 1584
Lenton, Francis. *Characterismi.* 1631
– *The young gallants whirligigg* ... 1629
M.,W. *The Man in the moone ...,* or the English Fortune-teller. 1609
Middleton, Thomas. *The Ant and the Nightingale.* In *The Works of Thomas Middleton*, ed. A.H. Bullen. 8 vols. London, 1885–6
M[un], T[homas]. *A Discovrse of Trade, From England vnto the East-Indies* ... 1621
Niccholes, Alexander. *A Discourse, of Marriage and Wiving.* 1615
Nixon, Anthony. *A Straunge Foot-Post* ... 1613
Overbury, Sir Thomas. *A Wife. Now the Widdow of Sir Tho: Overburye* ... 1614
Perkins, William. *The Reformation of Couetousnesse* ... 1603

Powell, Thomas. *The art of Thriving. Or, The plaine path-way to Preferment* ... 1635

Rawlidge, Richard. *A Monster Late Fovnd ovt and Discovered* ... Amsterdam, 1628

Rich, Barnaby. *The excellency of good woman.* 1613
– *Favltes Favlts, and nothing else but Favltes.* 1606
– *My Ladies Looking Glasse* ... 1616

Rollins, Hyder Edward, ed. *The Pepys Ballads.* 8 vols. Cambridge, Mass., 1929–32

Rowlands, Samuel, *The Knave of Clubbes.* 1609
– *The Knave of Harts* ... 1612
– *Looke to it: For, Ile Stabbe ye* ... 1604
– *More knaves yet? the knaves of spades and diamonds.* 1613

Rye, W.B., ed. *England as Seen by Foreigners in the Days of Elizabeth and James I.* 1865

The Skilfull Mountebanke, Or, Come, and I'le cure you. 1638

Smith, Henry. *The Examination of Vsurie.* 1591
– *A preparatiue to Mariage.* In *The Sermons of Maister Henrie Smith, gathered into one volume.* 1593

Snawsell, Robert. *A Looking Glasse for Maried Folkes* ... 1610

Stow, John. *A Survay of London*, ed. Henry Morley. 1890

Stubbes, Philip. *The Anatomie of Abuses*, ed. F.J. Furnivall. New Shakspere Society, Series VI. 1897–9
– *A Christal Glasse for Christian Women* ... 1592

Swetnam, Joseph. *The Araignment of Lewd, idle, froward, and vnconstant women* ... 1615

Tell-Trothes New-yeares Gift, ed. F.J. Furnivall. New Shakspere Society, Series VI, no. 2. 1876

Tilley, Morris Palmer, ed. *A Dictionary of Proverbs in England in the Sixteenth and Seventeenth Centuries.* Ann Arbor, 1950

Whately, William. *A Bride-Bush, or a Wedding Sermon* ... 1619

Whetstone, George. *A Mirovr for Magestrates of Cyties* ... *and* ... *a Touchstone for the Time.* 1584

Wilson, Thomas. *A Discourse upon Usury*, intro. R.H. Tawney. 1925

MODERN SCHOLARSHIP AND CRITICISM

Appleton, William W. *Beaumont and Fletcher: a Critical Study.* London, 1956

Bald, R.C. 'The Sources of Middleton's City Comedies,' *JEGP*, XXXIII (July 1934), 373–87

Barker, Richard Hindry. *Thomas Middleton.* New York, 1958

Barish, Jonas A. 'Bartholomew Fair and its Puppets,' *MLQ*, xx (March 1959), 3–17.

Barish, Jonas A., ed. *Ben Jonson: a Collection of Critical Essays*. Englewood Cliffs, N.J., 1963

Baskervill, Charles Read. *English Elements in Jonson's Early Comedy*. Austin, Texas, 1911

– 'Mummers' Wooing Plays in England,' *MP*, xxi (February 1924), 225–72

– 'The Sources and Analogues of *How a Man May Choose a Good Wife from a Bad*,' *PMLA*, xxiv, New Series xvii (December 1909), 711–30

Baum, Helena Watts. *The Satiric and the Didactic in Ben Jonson's Comedy*. Chapel Hill, 1947

Bentley, G.E. *The Jacobean and Caroline Stage*. 7 vols. Oxford, 1941–68

Berlin, Normand. 'Thomas Dekker: a Partial Reappraisal,' *SEL*, vi (Spring 1966), 263–77

Blayney, Glenn H. 'The Enforcement of Marriage in English Drama 1600–50,' *PQ*, xxxviii (October 1959), 459–72

Blissett, William. 'The Venter Tripartite in *The Alchemist*,' *SEL*, viii (Spring 1968), 323–34

Boas, F.S. *Thomas Heywood*. London, 1950

– *University Drama in the Tudor Age*. Oxford, 1914

Bond, R. Warwick, ed. *Early Plays from the Italian*. Oxford, 1911

Bradbrook, M.C. *The Growth and Structure of Elizabethan Comedy*. Harmondsworth, 1963

Brown, Arthur. 'Citizen Comedy and Domestic Drama,' in Brown and Harris, *Jacobean Theatre* (q.v.)

Brown, John Russell. *Shakespeare and his Comedies*. Second edition, London, 1962

Brown, John Russell, and Bernard Harris, eds. *Stratford-upon-Avon Studies I: Jacobean Theatre*. London, 1960

Camden, Carroll. *The Elizabethan Woman*. London, 1952

Doebler, John. 'Beaumont's *The Knight of the Burning Pestle* and the Prodigal Son Plays,' *SEL*, v (Spring 1965), 333–44

Donaldson, Ian. *The World Turned Upside-Down*. Oxford, 1970

Doran, Madeleine. *Endeavors of Art: a Study of Form in Elizabethan Drama*. Madison, Wisconsin, 1954

Dunkel, Wilbur D. *The Dramatic Technique of Thomas Middleton in his Comedies of London Life*. Chicago, 1925

Dunn, Esther C. *Ben Jonson's Art: Elizabethan Life and Literature as Reflected Therein*. Northampton, Mass., 1925

Dunn, T.A. *Philip Massinger: The Man and the Playwright*. Edinburgh, 1957

Eliot, T.S. *Elizabethan Dramatists*. London, 1962

Ellis-Fermor, Una M. *The Jacobean Drama*. London, 1958

Enck, John J. *Jonson and the Comic Truth*. Madison, Wisconsin, 1957

Enright, D.J. 'Elizabethan and Jacobean Comedy.' In *The Pelican Guide to English Literature, Vol. III: The Age of Shakespeare*, ed. Boris Ford. Harmondsworth, 1964

– 'Poetic Satire and Satire in Verse,' *Scrutiny*, XVIII (Winter 1951–2), 211–23

Evans, Bertrand. *Shakespeare's Comedies*. Oxford, 1960

Finkelpearl, Philip J. *John Marston of the Middle Temple*. Cambridge, Mass., 1969

Fisher, Margery. 'Notes on the Sources of Some Incidents in Middleton's London Plays,' *RES*, xv (July 1939), 283–93

Frye, Northrop. 'The Argument of Comedy,' *English Institute Essays, 1948*. New York, 1949

Gibbons, Brian. *Jacobean City Comedy*. London, 1968

Goodman, Paul. 'Comic Plots: *The Alchemist*.' In Barish, *Ben Jonson* (*q.v.*)

Green, William. *Shakespeare's Merry Wives of Windsor*. Princeton, 1962

Grivelet, Michel. *Thomas Heywood et le Drame Domestique Elizabéthain*. Paris, 1957

Gross, Alan Gerald. 'Social Change and Philip Massinger,' *SEL*, VII (Spring 1967), 329–42

Hallett, Charles A. 'Middleton's Allwit: The Urban Cynic,' *MLQ*, xxx (December, 1969), 498–507

– 'Penitent Brothel, the Succubus and Parson's *Resolution*: a Reappraisal of Penitent's Position in Middleton's Canon,' *SP*, LXIX (January 1972), 72–86

Harbage, Alfred. *Shakespeare and the Rival Traditions*. New York, 1952

Heffner, Ray L., Jr. 'Unifying Symbols in the Comedy of Ben Jonson,' in Barish, *Ben Jonson*, (*q.v.*)

Herford, C.H. *Studies in the Literary Relations of England and Germany in the Sixteenth Century*. Cambridge, 1886

Herrick, Marvin T. *Italian Comedy in the Renaissance*. Urbana, Ill., 1960

– *Tragicomedy: Its Origin and Development in Italy, France and England*. Urbana, Ill., 1955

Hexter, J.H. *Reappraisals in History*. London, 1963

Hole, Christiana. *The English Housewife in the Seventeenth Century*. London, 1953

Holmes, David M. *The Art of Thomas Middleton*. Oxford, 1970

Hunt, Mary Leland. *Thomas Dekker: a Study*. New York, 1911

Hunter, G.K. 'English Folly and Italian Vice: The Moral Landscape of John Marston,' in Brown and Harris, *Jacobean Theatre* (*q.v.*)

Jackson, Gabrielle Bernhard. *Vision and Judgment in Ben Jonson's Drama.* New Haven, 1968

Jones, Myrddin. 'Sir Epicure Mammon: A Study in "Spiritual Fornication,"' *Renaissance Quarterly*, xxii (Autumn 1969), 233–42

Jones-Davies, Marie-Thérèse. *Un Peintre de la Vie Londonienne: Thomas Dekker.* 2 vols. Paris, 1958

Kaplan, Joel H. 'Dramatic and Moral Energy in Ben Jonson's *Bartholomew Fair*,' *Renaissance Drama*, New Series iii (1970), 137–56

– 'Virtue's Holiday: Thomas Dekker and Simon Eyre,' *Renaissance Drama*, New Series ii (1969), 103–22

Knights, L.C. *Drama and Society in the Age of Jonson.* Harmondsworth, 1962

Lea, K.M. *Italian Popular Comedy.* 2 vols. Oxford, 1934

Leech, Clifford. *The John Fletcher Plays.* London, 1962

Levin, Harry. 'An Introduction to Ben Jonson,' in Barish, *Ben Jonson (q.v.)*

Levin, Richard. *The Multiple Plot in English Renaissance Drama.* Chicago, 1971

Lynch, Kathleen M. *The Social Mode of Restoration Comedy.* New York, 1926

Manheim, Michael. 'The Construction of *The Shoemakers' Holiday*,' *SEL*, x (Spring 1970), 315–23

– 'The Thematic Structure of Dekker's *2 Honest Whore*,' *SEL*, v (Spring 1965), 363–81

Moore, John B. *The Comic and the Realistic in English Drama.* New York, 1925

Nosworthy, J.M. 'Henry Porter,' *English*, vi (Summer 1946), 65–9.

O'Connor, John J. 'The Chief Source of Marston's *Dutch Courtezan*,' *SP*, liv (October 1957), 509–15

Palmer, John. *Ben Jonson.* London, 1934

Parker, R.B. 'Middleton's Experiments with Comedy and Judgement,' in Brown and Harris, *Jacobean Theatre (q.v.)*

– 'The Themes and Staging of Bartholomew Fair,' *UTQ*, xxxix (July 1970), 293–309

Parrott, Thomas Marc. *Shakespearean Comedy.* New York, 1949

Partridge, Edward B. *The Broken Compass.* London, 1958

– 'The Symbolism of Clothes in Jonson's Last Plays,' *JEGP*, lvi (1957), 396–409

Peery, William. 'The Influence of Jonson on Nathan Field,' *SP*, xliii (July 1946), 482–97

– 'The Portayal of Women in the Comedies of Nathan Field,' *Shakespeare Association Bulletin*, xxi (July 1946), 129–41

Peter, John. 'John Marston's Plays,' *Scrutiny*, xvii (Summer 1950), 132–53

Powell, C.L. *English Domestic Relations 1487–1653.* New York, 1917

Presson, Robert K. 'Marston's *Dutch Courtezan*: The Study of an Attitude in Adaptation,' *JEGP*, LV (1956), 403–16

Robinson, James E. '*Bartholomew Fair*: Comedy of Vapours,' *SEL*, I (Spring 1961), 65–80

Saintsbury, George. *A History of Elizabethan Literature*. London, 1887

Sale, Arthur. 'Introduction to *Every Man in his Humour*,' in Barish, *Ben Jonson (q.v.)*

Salingar, L.G. 'Farce and Fashion in "The Silent Woman,"' *Essays and Studies*, New Series XX (1967), 29–46

Schelling, Felix E. *Elizabethan Drama 1558–1642*. 2 vols. New York, 1959

Schoenbaum, Samuel. '*A Chaste Maid in Cheapside* and Middleton'sCity Comedy,' *Studies in the English Renaissance Drama*, ed. J.W. Bennett *et al*. New York, 1959

– 'The Precarious Balance of John Marston,' *PMLA*, LXVII (December 1952), 1069–78

Simpson, Percy. 'The Art of Ben Jonson,' *Essays and Studies*, XXX (1945)

Spencer, Theodore. 'John Marston,' *Criterion*, XIII (1934), 581–99

Stoll, Elmer Edgar. 'The Influence of Jonson on Dekker,' *MLN*, XXI (January 1906), 20–3

– *John Webster: the Periods of his Work Determined by his Relations to the Drama of his Day*. Boston, 1905

Stone, Lawrence. *The Crisis of the Aristocracy 1558–1641*. Oxford, 1965

Stone, Lawrence, ed. *Social Change and Revolution in England 1540–1640*. London, 1965

Stonex, Arthur Bivins. 'The Usurer in Elizabethan Drama,' *PMLA*, XXXI, New Series XXIV (June 1916), 190–210

Swinburne, A.C. *The Age of Shakespeare*. London, 1908

Tawney, R.H. *Religion and the Rise of Capitalism*. Harmondsworth, 1961

Thayer, C.G. *Ben Jonson: Studies in the Plays*. Norman, Oklahoma, 1963

Thorndike, Ashley H. *English Comedy*. New York, 1929

Tomlinson, T.B. *A Study of Elizabethan and Jacobean Tragedy*. Cambridge, 1964

Townsend, Freda L. *Apologie for Bartholmew Fayre: The Art of Jonson's Comedies*. New York, 1947

Trevelyan, G.M. *Illustrated English Social History, Vol. II: The Age of Shakespeare and the Stuart Period*. Harmondsworth, 1964

Ure, Peter. 'Patient Madman and Honest Whore: The Middleton-Dekker Oxymoron,' *Essays and Studies*, New Series, XIX (1966), 18–40

Velte, Mowbray. *The Bourgeois Elements in the Dramas of Thomas Heywood*. Mysore, 1922

Wallis, Lawrence Bergman. *Fletcher, Beaumont, and Company: Entertainers to the Jacobean Gentry.* New York, 1947

Wells, Henry W. *Elizabethan and Jacobean Playwrights.* New York, 1939

Williams, Robert I. 'Machiavelli's *Mandragola,* Touchwood Senior, and the Comedy of Middleton's *A Chaste Maid in Cheapside,*' *SEL,* x (Spring 1970) 385–96

Wilson, John Dover. *Shakespeare's Happy Comedies.* London, 1962

Wilson, F.P. *Elizabethan and Jacobean.* Oxford, 1945

Wright, Celeste Turner. 'Some Conventions Regarding the Usurer in Elizabethan Literature,' *SP,* xxxi (April 1934), 176–97

Wright, Louis B. *Middle-Class Culture in Elizabethan England.* Chapel Hill, N.C. 1935

– 'Social Aspects of Some Belated Moralities,' *Anglia,* LIV (1930), 107–48

Zall, Paul M. 'John Marston, Moralist,' *ELH,* xx (September 1953), 186–93

Index